Best Editorial Cartoons of the Year

DICK WALLMEYER
Courtesy Long Beach Press-Telegram

BEST EDITORIAL CARTOONS OF THE YEAR

1988 EDITION

Edited by
CHARLES BROOKS

PELICAN PUBLISHING COMPANY
Gretna 1988

Library of Congress Serial Catalog Data

Best editorial cartoons. 1972-
    Gretna [La.] Pelican Pub. Co.
    v. 29 cm. annual-
"A pictorial history of the year."

    1. United States- Politics and government—
1969—Caricatures and Cartoons—Periodicals.
E839.5.B45   320.9'7309240207   73-643645
ISSN 0091-2220   MARC-S

Manufactured in the United States of America
Published by Pelican Publishing Company, Inc.
1101 Monroe Street, Gretna, Louisiana 70053

Contents

Award-Winning Cartoons

1987 NATIONAL HEADLINERS CLUB AWARD

MIKE PETERS
Editorial Cartoonist
Dayton Daily News

Native of St. Louis, Missouri; earned bachelor of arts from Washington University, 1965; editorial cartoonist for the Chicago *Daily News,* 1965-69; editorial cartoonist for the Dayton, Ohio *Daily News,* 1969 to the present; syndicated by United Features Syndicate; author of three cartoon books; previous winner of National Headliner Award, 1982; winner of Pulitzer Prize for cartooning, 1981, and the Sigma Delta Chi Award, 1985.

1987 PULITZER PRIZE

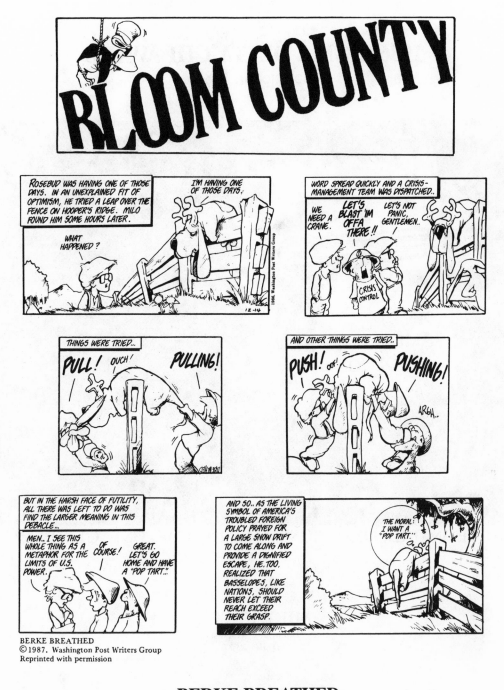

BERKE BREATHED
Cartoonist
Washington Post Writers Group

Born in Los Angeles, 1957; graduate of the University of Texas, with a degree in photojournalism; drew first political cartoon in 1977; first cartoon evolved into a college comic strip, "The Academia Waltz;" launched "Bloom County" into national syndication in 1980 with the Washington Post Writers Group; four book collections of his comics have been published.

1986 SIGMA DELTA CHI AWARD
(Selected in 1987)

THE EDMOND, OKLAHOMA MEMORIAL POSTAGE STAMP

MIKE KEEFE
Editorial Cartoonist
Denver Post

Born in Santa Rosa, California, 1946; holds two degrees in mathematics from the University of Missouri at Kansas City and has completed coursework for the doctorate; editorial cartoonist for the Denver *Post,* 1975 to the present; syndicated nationally by the North America Syndicate; co-creator, with Tim Menees, of the comic strip "Iota," distributed by Universal Press Syndicate.

1987 FISCHETTI AWARD

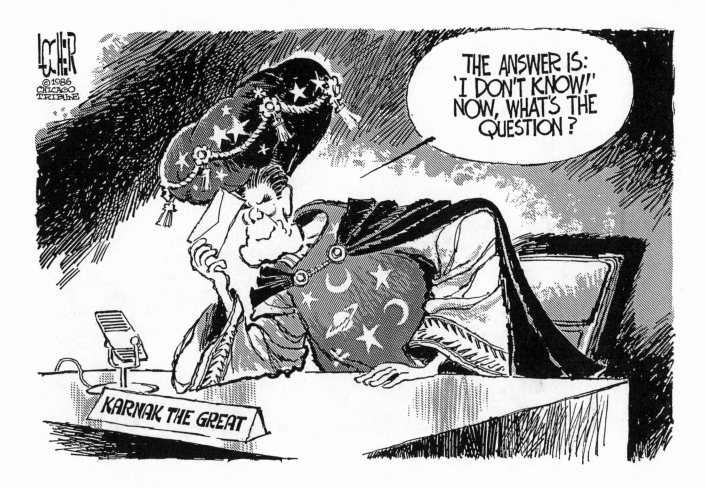

DICK LOCHER
Editorial Cartoonist
Chicago Tribune

Born in Dubuque, Iowa, 1929; attented Loras College and the University of Iowa; studied art at the Chicago Academy of Fine Art and the Art Center of Los Angeles; assistant to Chester Gould, creator of the Dick Tracy comic strip, 1957-1961; cartoonist for Dick Tracy comic strip, 1983 to present; editorial cartoonist, Chicago *Tribune*, 1973 to present; syndicated by the Chicago *Tribune;* winner of the Pulitzer Prize, the Sigma Delta Chi Award, and the Overseas Press Club Award for cartooning, in one year, 1983; illustrator of *Flying Can Be Fun,* By Michael Kilian.

1986 NATIONAL NEWSPAPER AWARD/CANADA
(Selected in 1987)

BRIAN GABLE
Editorial Cartoonist
Regina Leader-Post

Born in Saskatoon, 1949; earned a degree in fine arts from the University of Saskatchewan and a bachelor of education degree from the University of Toronto; high school teacher in Brockville, Ontario, 1971-80; editorial cartoonist for the Regina *Leader Post,* 1980-87; editorial cartoonist for the Toronto *Globe and Mail,* 1987 to the present.

Best Editorial Cartoons of the Year

**'Golly, I Can Hardly Wait Until
The Investigating Board Tells Us How This Happened'**

TOM ENGELHARDT
Courtesy St. Louis Post-Dispatch

The Reagan Administration

When the Contra Connection was revealed in the sale of arms by the U.S. to Iran, President Reagan appointed the Tower Commission to investigate the affair. After lengthy study, the commission handed down a harsh indictment of President Reagan's methods of management, picturing him as confused and out of touch with vital governmental programs.

In July, Reagan nominated Robert Bork to the U.S. Supreme Court, but a massive lobbying campaign against him by liberals resulted in a Senate vote of 58 to 42 against confirmation.

There were charges during the year that Nancy Reagan was the real power behind the President. It was reported widely that she engineered the replacing of White House Chief of Staff Donald Regan with former Senator Howard Baker.

Attorney General Edwin Meese found himself in hot water when questions were raised concerning his competence and character in connection with the Iran-Contra scandal and in a probe of corruption in a New York business firm he had attempted to help. Furthermore, Meese had pushed strongly for Bork's nomination to the Supreme Court. After Bork's nomination was defeated, Meese backed another conservative, Douglas Ginsburg. The Senate defeat of these two nominees was widely regarded as a reflection on Meese.

ROY PETERSON
Courtesy Vancouver Sun

"BUT HE DIDN'T GROVEL AND CRAWL"

©1987 FORT WORTH STAR-TELEGRAM — ETTA HULME NEA

TOWER COMMISSION REPORT: THE CLOTHES HAVE NO EMPEROR

EDD ULUSCHAK
©Southam Syndicate

STEVE SACK
Courtesy Minneapolis Star-Tribune

16

MILT PRIGGEE
Courtesy Spokane Chronicle

JIM BERRY
©NEA

DICK GIBSON
Courtesy Toronto Sun

BOB TAYLOR
Courtesy Dallas Times-Herald

17

Teflon No More

JIM BORGMAN
Courtesy Cincinnati Enquirer

"THERE'S THEM AS SAYS YOU SHOULDA WHIPPED 'IM WHEN 'E WAS ONLY 'ARF THIS BIG"

18

'In just a moment we'll know what the wise old man of the mountain
has to say'

CHARLES BISSELL
Courtesy The Tennessean

JERRY FEARING
Courtesy St. Paul Pioneer Press

"DAT'S WHAT I LIKE ABOUT THE PRESIDENT..., HE BELIEVES IN THE PRIVATE SECTOR"

WALT HANDELSMAN
Courtesy Scranton Times

MIKE THOMPSON
© Thompson Cartoons

THE MEESE FILES

SANDY CAMPBELL
Courtesy The Tennessean

MIKE LUCKOVICH
Courtesy Times-Picayune (New Orleans)

ROY PETERSON
Courtesy Vancouver Sun

The Presidential Candidates

During 1987, candidates for the highest office in the land continued to have trouble getting people to listen. On the Democratic side, the two leading in the polls, Gary Hart and Jesse Jackson, were considered by many to be "unelectable." Hart had withdrawn earlier in the year because of his involvement with model Donna Rice. Then, in December, he suddenly announced that he was back in the race.

Of the "seven dwarfs," as critics labeled them, Jackson was the only one to generally reach the 20 percent mark in the polls. Rep. Patricia Schroeder withdrew from the race in September, as did Sen. Joseph Biden. Biden was presiding over the confirmation hearings of Robert Bork for supreme court justice, when a series of stories broke revealing plagiarism on his part in several speeches and a law school paper.

Candidates Michael Dukakis (Mass.), Albert Gore, Jr. (Tenn.), Paul Simon (Ill.), nor Richard Gephardt (Mo.) seemed to be lighting a spark among voters as the year drew to a close.

On the Republican side, Vice-President George Bush seemed to be leading in the polls, with Bob Dole in second place. Following the two leaders in the polls, with 10 percent or less, were: former Secretary of State Alexander Haig, Rep. Jack Kemp (N.Y.), the Rev. Pat Robertson, and former Delaware Governor Pierre duPont IV.

WILEY
Courtesy San Francisco Examiner

C. S. WELLS
Courtesy Augusta Chronicle

BILL GARNER
Courtesy Washington Times

DANA SUMMERS
Courtesy Orlando Sentinel

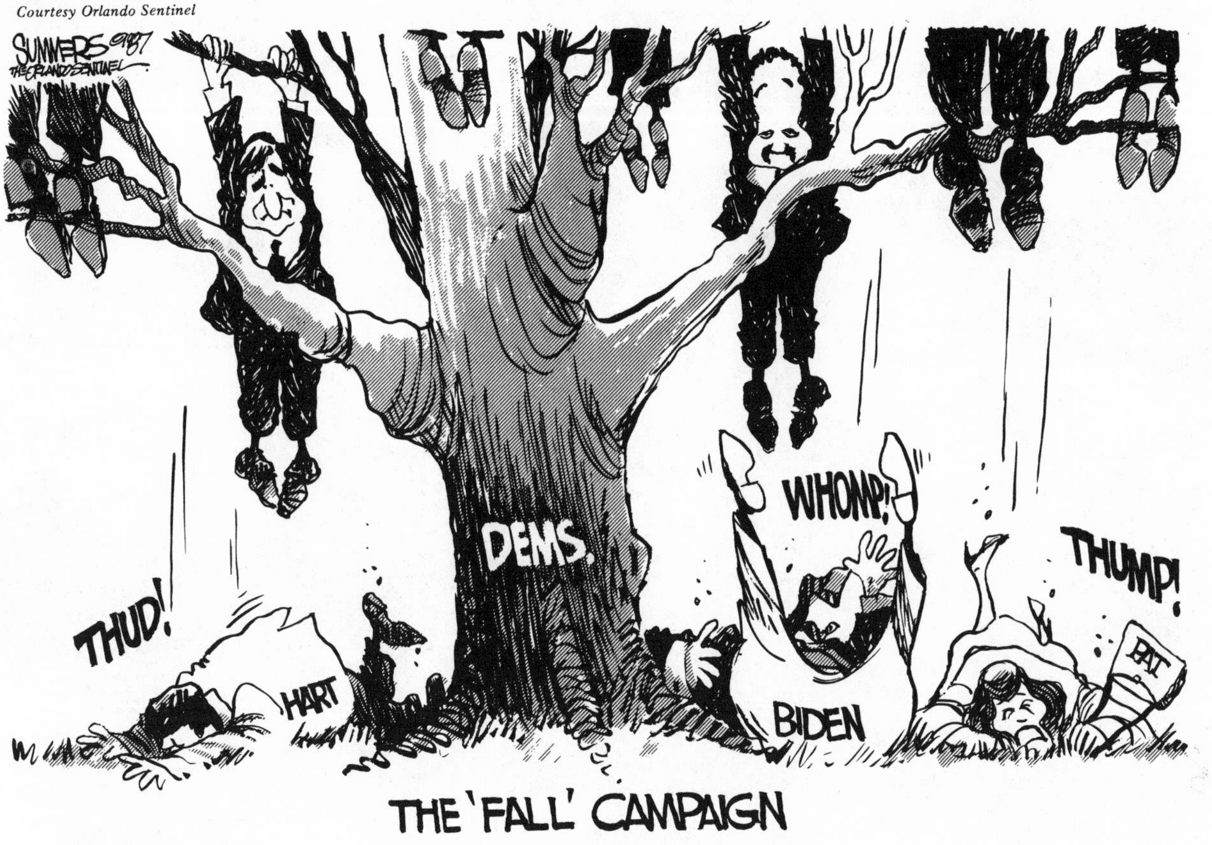
SUMMERS ©1987 THE ORLANDO SENTINEL
DEMS.
THUD!
HART
WHOMP!
BIDEN
THUMP!
PAT
THE 'FALL' CAMPAIGN

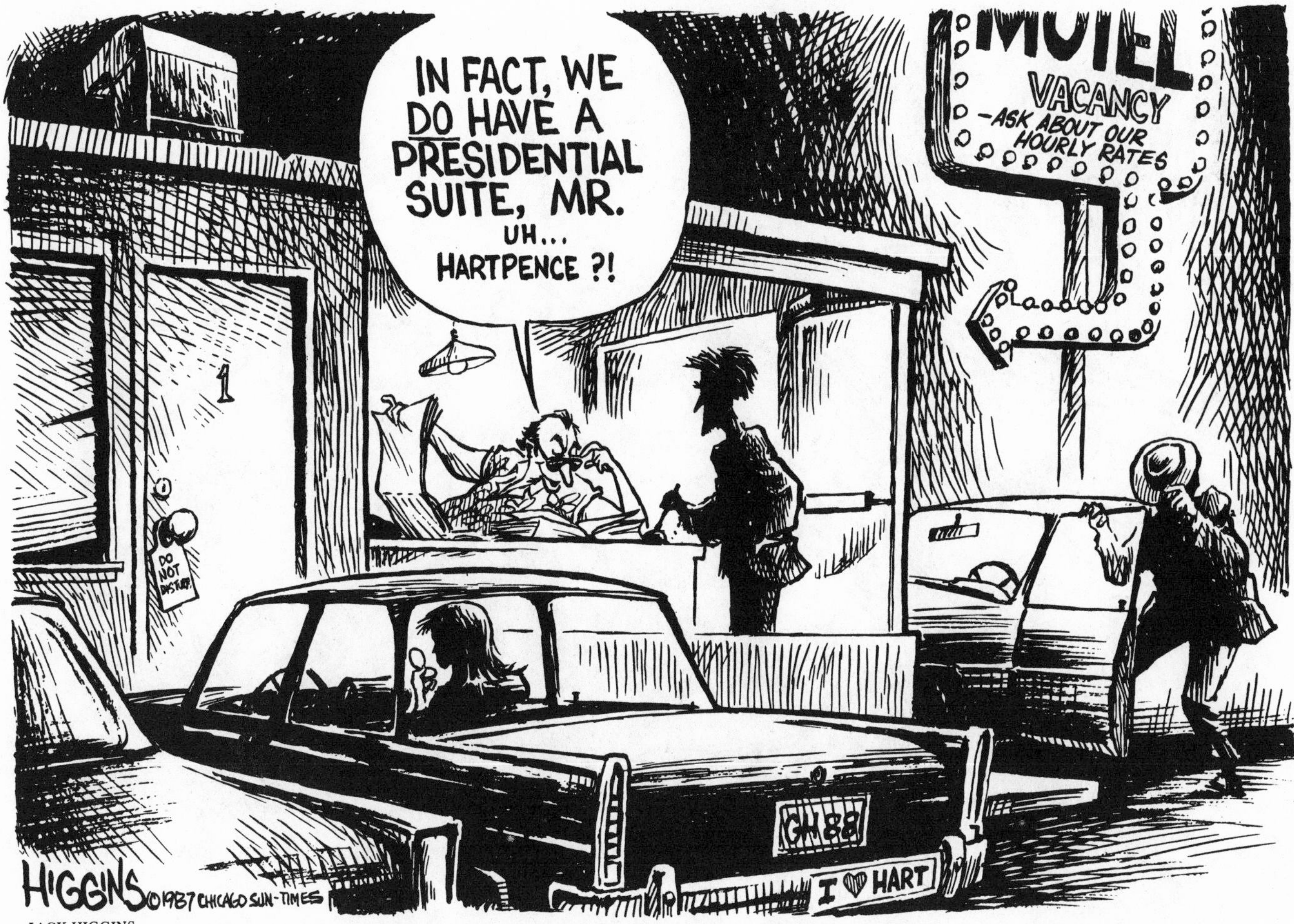
MOTEL
VACANCY
-ASK ABOUT OUR HOURLY RATES
IN FACT, WE DO HAVE A PRESIDENTIAL SUITE, MR. UH... HARTPENCE ?!
1
DO NOT DISTURB
GH 88
I ♥ HART
HIGGINS ©1987 CHICAGO SUN-TIMES

JACK HIGGINS
Courtesy Chicago Sun-Times

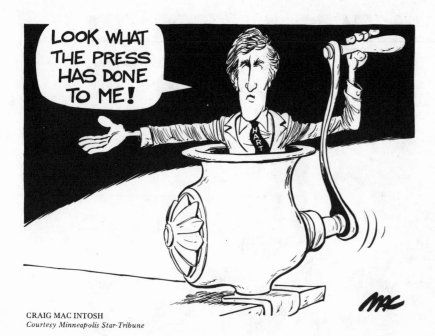

CRAIG MAC INTOSH
Courtesy Minneapolis Star-Tribune

JIM BERRY
©NEA

BRUCE BEATTIE
Courtesy Daytona Beach News-Journal

LARRY WRIGHT
Courtesy Detroit News

BOB GORRELL
Courtesy Richmond News Leader

JOHN CRAWFORD
Courtesy Alabama Journal

27

TOM GIBB
Courtesy Altoona Mirror

RANDY R. WICKS
Courtesy The Signal (Newhall, Calif.)

JIM BORGMAN
Courtesy Cincinnati Enquirer

MILT PRIGGEE
Courtesy Spokane Chronicle

THE TORCH IS PASSED...

SCOTT WILLIS
Courtesy San Jose Mercury-News

DICK WRIGHT
Courtesy Providence Journal-Bulletin

GARY HUCK
©U E News

TOM GIBB
Courtesy Altoona Mirror

30

HY ROSEN
Courtesy Albany Times Union

DAN WASSERMAN
Courtesy Boston Globe

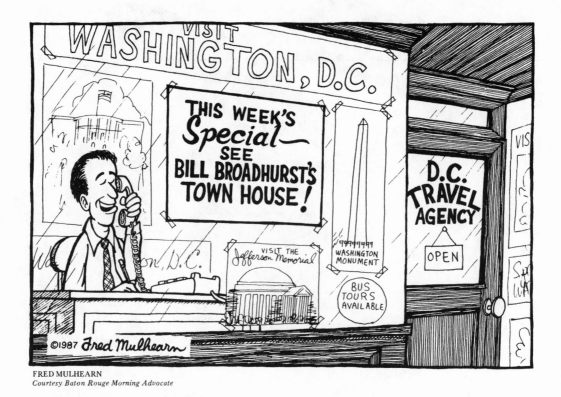

FRED MULHEARN
Courtesy Baton Rouge Morning Advocate

MIKE KEEFE
Courtesy Denver Post

The Mideast

The Iran-Iraq war ended its seventh year in September, and the military balance remained roughly the same. In May, Iraq-U.S. relations were strained by an Iraq attack on the U.S. warship *Stark*. The incident did no lasting damage to the relationship, however, and actually may have benefited it.

The Persian Gulf, the major waterway for oil shipments from the Mideast as well as the battleground for much of the Iran-Iraq war, held the attention of the world during 1987. Ships from the U.S., the U.S.S.R., and Western Europe cruised the waters in an attempt to protect civilian shipping. Kuwait asked the U.S. for protection in July, and the U.S. responded with warships. It also reflagged Kuwaiti tankers with the Stars and Stripes.

The sale of arms to Iran in an effort to open up relations with that country—and to seek the release of American hostages—created an uproar around the world. Many nations, however, including some in the West, continued to sell arms to various governments in the Mideast.

JIMMY MARGULIES
Courtesy Houston Post

" All those in favor of telling Iran and Iraq to stop using the weapons we sell them..."

MIKE KEEFE
Courtesy Denver Post

DAN WASSERMAN
Courtesy Boston Globe

JON KENNEDY
Courtesy Arkansas Democrat

Old familiar feeling

ROB ROGERS
Courtesy Pittsburgh Press

DON PLETCHER
Rothco

EDGAR SOLLER
Courtesy World Reporter

ANOTHER JOB FOR ESCORTMAN

DAVE FITZSIMMONS
Courtesy Arizona Daily Star

ED FISCHER
Courtesy Rochester Post-Bulletin

BOB DORNFRIED
© Rothco

BOB TAYLOR
Courtesy Dallas Times-Herald

TOM ADDISON
Courtesy The (Williamston, S.C.) Journal

I Got The Idea From Our Ships

Showing the Flag.

RANAN LURIE
©Cartoonews International

UFO'S

THE LOCH NESS MONSTER

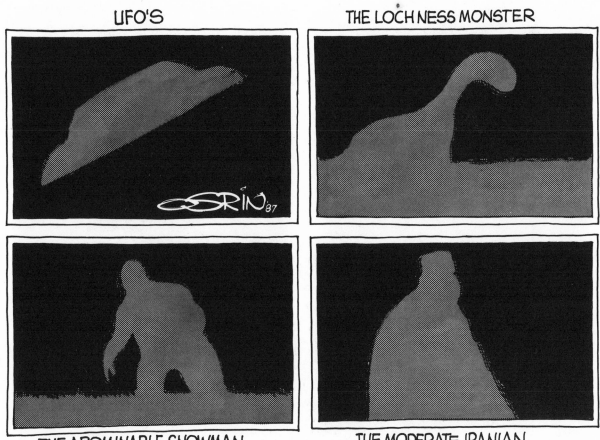

THE ABOMINABLE SNOWMAN

THE MODERATE IRANIAN

RAY OSRIN
Courtesy Cleveland Plain Dealer

39

JOHN TREVER
Courtesy Albuquerque Journal

"HURRY!... BEFORE THE RUSSIANS GET HERE!"

LAZARO FRESQUET
Courtesy El Miami Herald

TOM ENGELHARDT
Courtesy St. Louis Post-Dispatch

**'I've Got The Red And White Stripes Painted On —
Now, Where Do The Stars Go?'**

LAMBERT DER
Courtesy Greenville News

40

Foreign Affairs

The ruling Nationalist Party and President Pieter W. Botha were returned to office in South African elections on May 6. The government arrested leading anti-apartheid activists, passed restrictive new laws, and continued to use force in keeping order in the black areas of the country.

More Western businesses moved their operations from South Africa as pressures from other parts of the world mounted. Exxon, which had pulled out in December of 1986, was followed by Dow Chemical, Citicorp, ITT, Kentucky Fried Chicken, McGraw-Hill, and Ford Motor Company. During the past two years more than 130 businesses have abandoned South Africa.

Philippine President Corazon Aquino faced problems from all sides during the year, including a bloody coup attempt in which 53 people were killed and 300 injured. Meanwhile, deposed President Ferdinand Marcos continued to dream of returning to power. Pope John Paul II drew protests from around the world when he granted an audience to Austrian President Kurt Waldheim, who was accused of participating in Nazi atrocities during World War II.

Britain's Margaret Thatcher won a third consecutive term, the longest reign by a British prime minister in more than 150 years. She is credited with having slowly turned Britain back from the path of socialism.

RANAN LURIE
©Cartoonews International

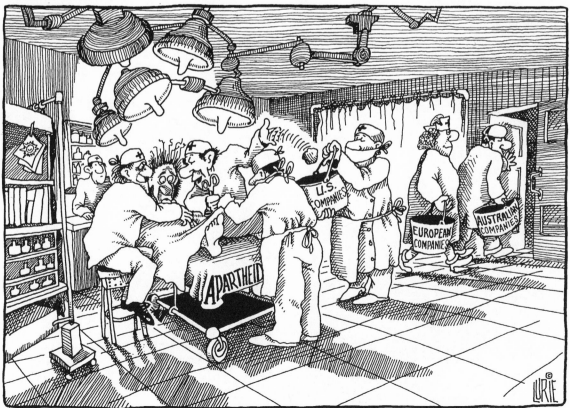

"Congratulations. Your parts are being donated to better causes."

41

THE CAT THAT SWALLOWED THE CANARY

DAVE GRANLUND
Courtesy Middlesex (Mass.) News

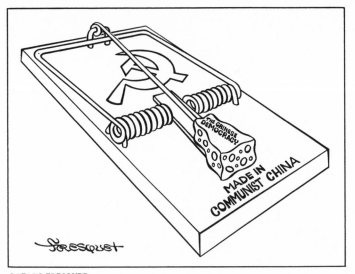

LAZARO FRESQUET
Courtesy El Miami Herald

SANDY CAMPBELL
Courtesy The Tennessean

DICK GIBSON
Courtesy Toronto Sun

RAY OSRIN
Courtesy Cleveland Plain Dealer

CRAIG MAC INTOSH
Courtesy Minneapolis Star-Tribune

CHUCK ASAY
Courtesy Colorado Springs Gazette

Iran-Contra Hearings

In late 1986 the stunning news broke that Robert McFarlane, President Reagan's national security advisor from 1983 to 1985, had delivered a planeload of arms to Iran's Ayatollah Khomeini. The Reagan Administration had insisted repeatedly that it would not make concessions to terrorists and had urged allies to follow suit.

In January of 1987, both houses of Congress named select committees to investigate the affair, and hearings were televised nationally from May to August of 1987. The man in the center seemed to be Marine Lt. Col. Oliver North, an aide to National Security Advisor John Poindexter. After six days of intensive grilling, North walked out of the hearings a folk hero to many Americans. His answers to the committee members' questions were sharp and clear, his manner was courteous, and he left the image of a "can do" Marine who did his best to save American hostages and combat communism.

The joint congressional panel issued its report in November, concluding that President Reagan did not know of the diversion of funds from the Iranian arms sale to the Contras in Nicaragua. But the report insisted that Reagan bore "the ultimate responsibility" for the actions of his subordinates, whether he knew of their actions or not. He was chastised for not fulfilling his constitutional duty "to take care that the laws be faithfully executed."

Lawrence E. Walsh was named independent counsel to investigate the affair for possible criminal violations.

TOM FLANNERY
Courtesy Baltimore Sun

"Looks Like Casey's Taking It With Him"

45

CLAY BENNETT
Courtesy St. Petersburg Times

MIKE SMITH
Courtesy Las Vegas Sun

THE FISH THAT GOT AWAY

GLENN FODEN
© Patuxent Publishing

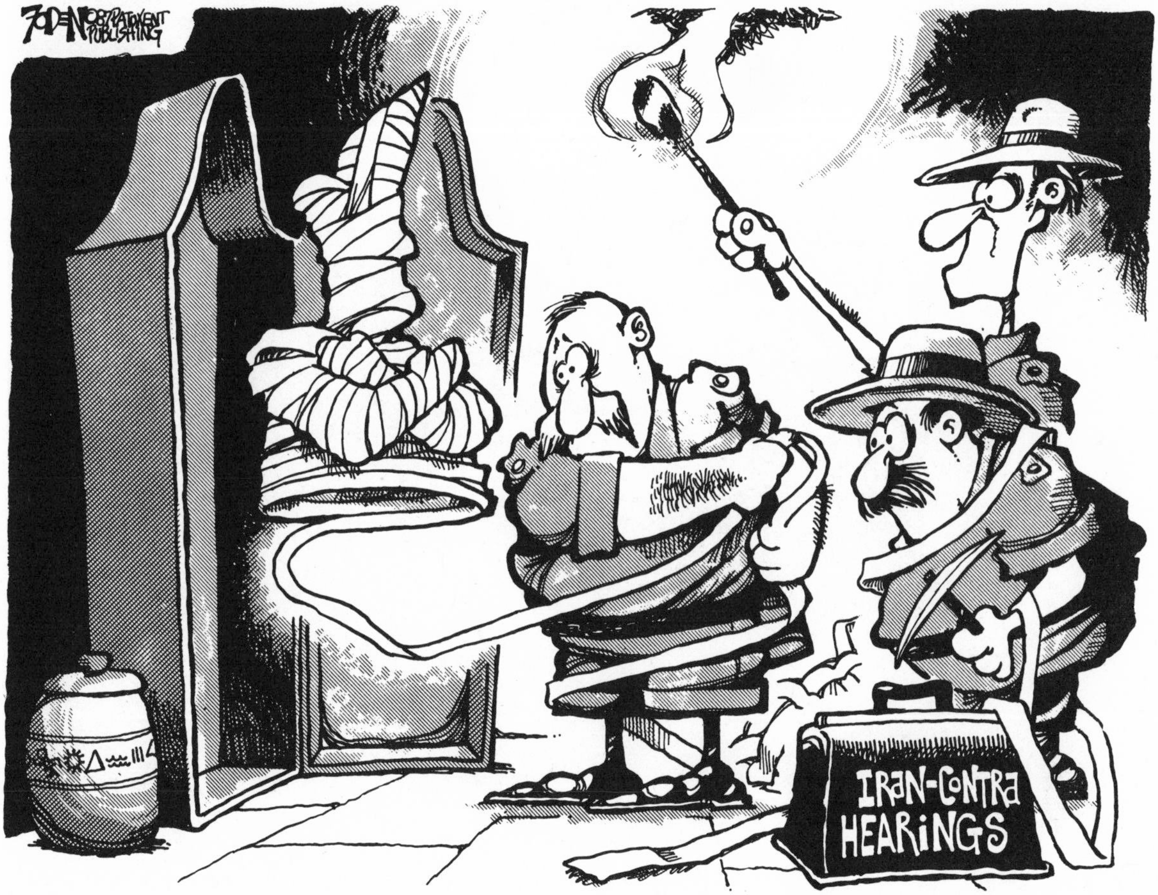
FODEN ©87 PATUXENT PUBLISHING
IRAN-CONTRA HEARINGS

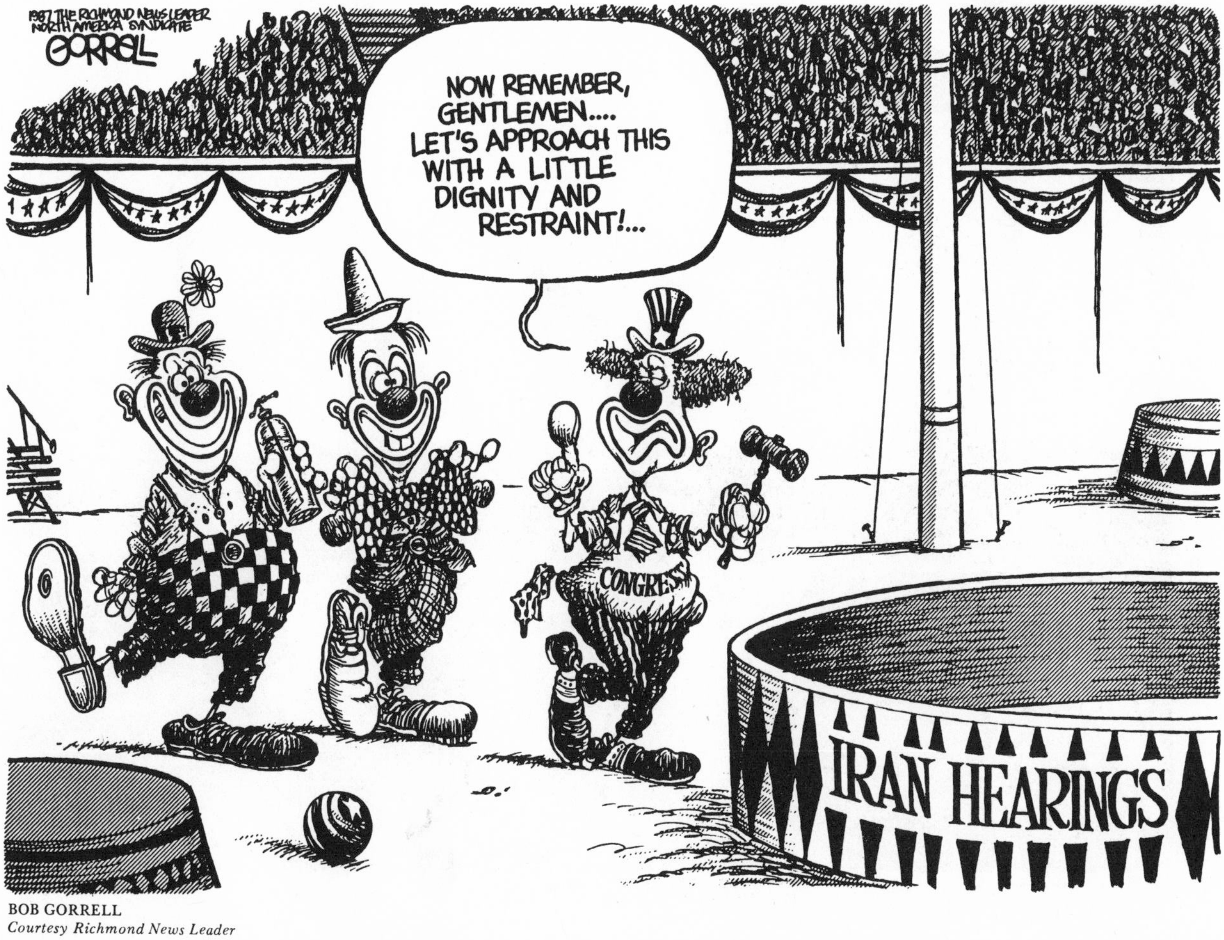
1987 THE RICHMOND NEWS LEADER NORTH AMERICA SYNDICATE
GORRELL
NOW REMEMBER, GENTLEMEN.... LET'S APPROACH THIS WITH A LITTLE DIGNITY AND RESTRAINT!...
CONGRESS
IRAN HEARINGS

BOB GORRELL
Courtesy Richmond News Leader

SANDY CAMPBELL
Courtesy The Tennessean

MICHAEL RAMIREZ
©Baker Communications

DRAPER HILL
Courtesy Detroit News

JIM BERRY
©NEA

JACK HIGGINS
Courtesy Chicago Sun-Times

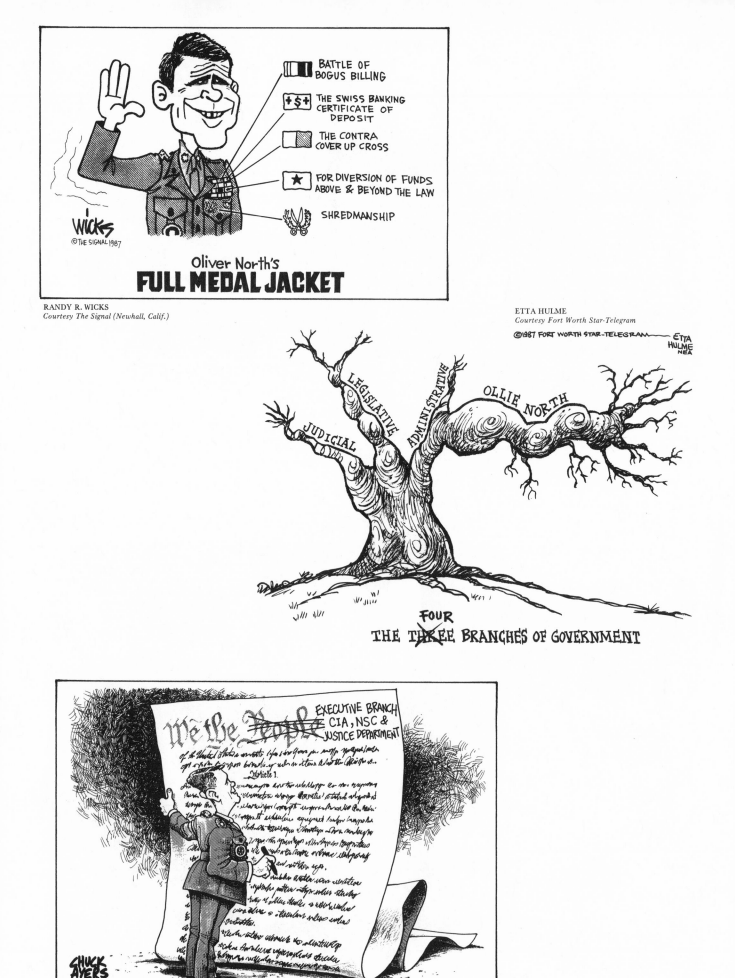

Oliver North's
FULL MEDAL JACKET

BATTLE OF
BOGUS BILLING

THE SWISS BANKING
CERTIFICATE OF
DEPOSIT

THE CONTRA
COVER UP CROSS

FOR DIVERSION OF FUNDS
ABOVE & BEYOND THE LAW

SHREDMANSHIP

WICKS
©THE SIGNAL 1987

RANDY R. WICKS
Courtesy The Signal (Newhall, Calif.)

ETTA HULME
Courtesy Fort Worth Star-Telegram

©1987 FORT WORTH STAR-TELEGRAM
ETTA HULME NEA

JUDICIAL
LEGISLATIVE
ADMINISTRATIVE
OLLIE NORTH

~~FOUR~~
THE ~~THREE~~ BRANCHES OF GOVERNMENT

We the ~~People~~
EXECUTIVE BRANCH
CIA, NSC &
JUSTICE DEPARTMENT

CHUCK AYERS
©1987 AKRON BEACON JOURNAL

50   CHUCK AYERS
Courtesy Akron Beacon-Journal

There Seems To Be A Loose Cannon--!!

IT WASN'T PART OF THE ARMS DEAL!

CHUCK WERNER
Courtesy Indianapolis Star

THE SMOKING GUN!

HUMAN CANNONBALL
ON TV!
SEE IT FREE!

CONGRESS

DID I HEAR A BACKFIRE?

JIM DOBBINS
Courtesy Winchester (Mass.) Union-Leader

MIKE SHELTON
Courtesy Orange County Register

"As far as I'm concerned, anyone who can get Jim and Tammy Bakker off the front page IS a national hero."

BRUCE BEATTIE
Courtesy Daytona Beach News-Journal

VIC HARVILLE
Courtesy Texarkana Gazette

STEVE LINDSTROM
Courtesy News-Tribune & Herald (Minn.)

PAUL SZEP
Courtesy Boston Globe

The Teflon Breakthrough

BOB TAYLOR
Courtesy Dallas Times-Herald

TOM CURTIS
©National Review

JIMMY MARGULIES
Courtesy Houston Post

SNAPSHOTS FROM ADMIRAL POINDEXTER'S PHOTOGRAPHIC MEMORY

LARRY WRIGHT
Courtesy Detroit News

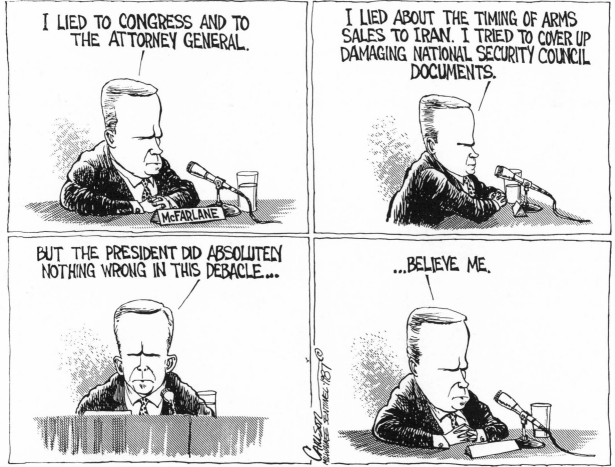

STUART CARLSON
Courtesy Milwaukee Sentinel

DAVE GRANLUND
Courtesy Middlesex (Mass.) News

Every little movement has a meaning all its own.

DRAPER HILL
Courtesy Detroit News

CASEY'S GHOST

KIRK WALTERS
Courtesy Toledo Blade

BOB SULLIVAN
Courtesy Worcester (Mass.) Telegram

HY ROSEN
Courtesy Albany Times Union

"TAKEN TO THE CLEANERS"

STEVE ARTLEY
©Extra Newspaper Features

Latin America

In Nicaragua, prospects for peace looked better in late 1987 when President Daniel Ortega and leaders of four other Central American nations signed a peace accord. Under the agreement, a cease-fire was declared, amnesty was given, and talks with rebels in each country were initiated.

The plan also called for a cutoff of outside aid to guerrilla groups and prohibited the use of the territory of one country for attacks on another nation. It further stipulated that each country was to have a free press and a democratic, pluralistic political system, and that state of emergency laws be lifted.

In Haiti, government violations of human rights continued under the Namphy regime just as it did under the Duvalier dictatorship. On July 29, ten Haitians were killed when soldiers fired on a peaceful demonstration. Ten days earlier, an estimated 250 peasants demanding land reform were massacred. And two party leaders were murdered late in the year, further feeding the flames of discontent and violence.

Election day, November 29, saw a wave of terrorist attacks, leaving dozens more dead. The election was canceled, and the electoral council was disbanded. The U.S. suspended practically all military aid and some economic aid to Haiti.

RAOUL HUNTER
Courtesy Le Soleil

UN AN APRÈS.

A YEAR AFTER

Which group wants to share in America's wealth, but refuses to learn our language?

A.

B.

FORM C
CLAUSE Z
CONNECT THE DOTS
MAZE B

IRS

MARGULIES
©1987 HOUSTON POST

JIMMY MARGULIES
Courtesy Houston Post

V. C. ROGERS
Courtesy Durham Morning Herald

Administration launches ICECAPP (Intra-Continental Emergency Central American Peace Plan).

Latin leaders respond with WIMPPP (Well-Intentioned Militarily Powerless Peace Package).

Sky-High Really Embarrassing Document Destroyer (SHREDD) intercepts WIMPPP, but not before...

... WIMPPP dislodges ICECAPP's tenuously attached booster COLDFOOT (Coalition Of Liberal Democrats Fearful Of Overseas Trouble).

This, coupled with the surprise disengagement of CONTRA (Counter-Ortega Non-Terrorist Rightist Alliance), causes the whole contraption to fall...

...on an elderly gentleman vacationing in Rancho del Cielo, California.

DICK WRIGHT
Courtesy Providence Journal-Bulletin

STEVEN TURTIL
Courtesy Charleston (W. Va.) Daily Mail

LEN BORO
Courtesy Phoenix Gazette

DENNIS RENAULT
Courtesy Sacramento Bee

JIM DOBBINS
Courtesy Winchester (Mass.) Union-Leader

National Defense

In South Korea, over 200,000 members of the South Korean and U.S. land, sea, and air forces took part in the annual "Team Spirit" joint defense exercise early in the year. Due to the approaching 1988 Olympic Games, U.S. support for South Korean security was reaffirmed at bilateral security sessions.

The two houses of Congress compromised on a bill funding U.S. defense spending at $296 billion if efforts to reduce the deficit were successful and $289 billion if not. President Reagan's Strategic Defense Initiative (SDI) received $3.9 billion.

In November, Caspar Weinberger announced his resignation as secretary of defense, citing personal reasons. He had been defense secretary since the beginning of the Reagan years. He was replaced by Frank C. Carlucci.

Under the December Summit agreement, reached in Washington, the Soviets will scrap four weapons to America's one—1,575 warheads on 680 launchers to 364 launchers with only one warhead each. The treaty to scrap medium-range missiles (INF) will destroy 2,600 warheads. It eliminates weapons that can hit Europe and the edges of the U.S.S.R.

MIKE KEEFE
Courtesy Denver Post

ETTA HULME
Courtesy Fort Worth Star-Telegram

STEVE KELLY
Courtesy San Diego Union

"HEY!... WHY DON'T WE BE MORE NEIGHBORLY AND REMOVE THIS FENCE?"

JOE HELLER
Courtesy Green Bay Press-Gazette

JERRY BYRD
Courtesy Beaumont Enterprise

$2 TRILLION MILITARY BUILDUP

CHEF CAP'S LEGACY - THE WEINBURGER

BILL MITCHELL
©Gannett Rochester Newspapers

BILL SANDERS
Courtesy Milwaukee Journal

MARTIN GARRITY
Courtesy Fair Oaks (Calif.) Post

GEORGE FISHER
Courtesy Arkansas Gazette

DICK WALLMEYER
Courtesy Long Beach Press-Telegram

STEVE GREENBERG
Courtesy Seattle Post-Intelligencer

The Soviet Union

Soviet leader Mikhail Gorbachev projected a dynamic and attractive image during a busy 1987. In the spring, for example, opinion polls in West Germany rated him as more concerned about peace than President Reagan. Gorbachev worked hard on one of his pet projects—*glasnost,* meaning openness—in Soviet society, and spurred efforts toward decentralization and increased competition in the U.S.S.R. economy.

Gorbachev faced increasing pressure from the U.S. and much of the Western world to pull Russian troops out of Afghanistan. He hinted the Soviets would be willing to begin troop withdrawals if the Reagan Administration would agree to stop supplying the Afghan rebels with arms.

In the fall Gorbachev disappeared from view for seven weeks amid speculation about his health and possible eroding authority. But it turned out he had been writing a book, *Perestroika: New Thinking for Our Country and the World.*

A young West German pilot, Mathias Rust, became an international figure in May when he flew a rented single-engine Cessna 172 more than 500 miles through heavily defended Russian air space and landed in Red Square in Moscow. The youth claimed to be promoting world peace, but the Soviets were unconvinced and sentenced Rust to four years in a labor camp.

CHUCK ASAY
Courtesy Colorado Springs Gazette

"RELAX AND FEEL THE POWER OF GLASNOST..."

MIKHAIL ATTEMPTS TO LIVEN UP THE PARTY

DICK WALLMEYER
Courtesy Long Beach Press-Telegram

ANOTHER DARING FLYER BUZZES THE KREMLIN

LOW-TECH STEALTH BOMBER

KIRK WALTERS
Courtesy Toledo Blade

JON KENNEDY
Courtesy Arkansas Democrat

For the world to see...

AISLIN
Courtesy Montreal Gazette

ART HENRIKSON
©Paddock Publications, Inc.

ED GAMBLE
Courtesy Florida Times-Union

"I'M OFF TO EUROPE ON ANOTHER PUBLIC RELATIONS TRIP...TRY TO KEEP THE NOISE DOWN, WILL YA!!"

Going All Out?

EDDIE GERMANO
Courtesy Brockton Enterprise

RAOUL HUNTER
Courtesy Le Soleil

JACK MC LEOD
© Army Times

MARK CULLUM
Courtesy Birmingham News

STEVEN TURTIL
Courtesy Charleston (W. Va.) Daily Mail

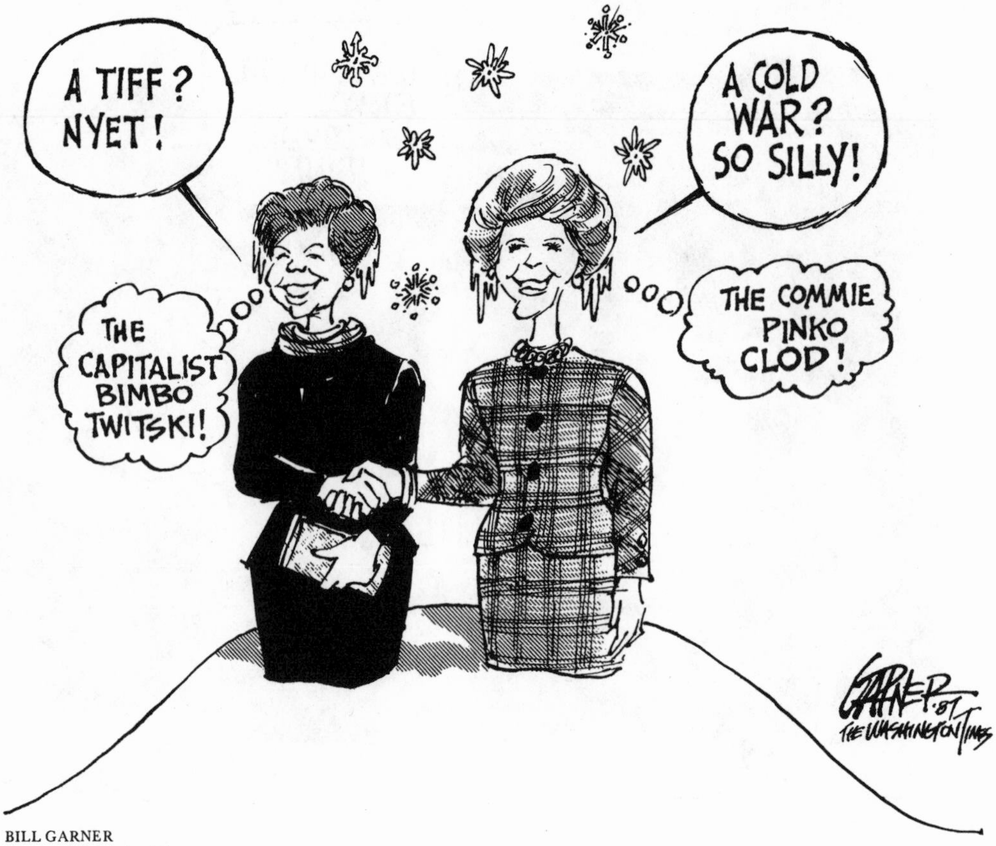
A TIFF? NYET!
THE CAPITALIST BIMBO TWITSKI!
A COLD WAR? SO SILLY!
THE COMMIE PINKO CLOD!
GARNER '87 THE WASHINGTON TIMES

BILL GARNER
Courtesy Washington Times

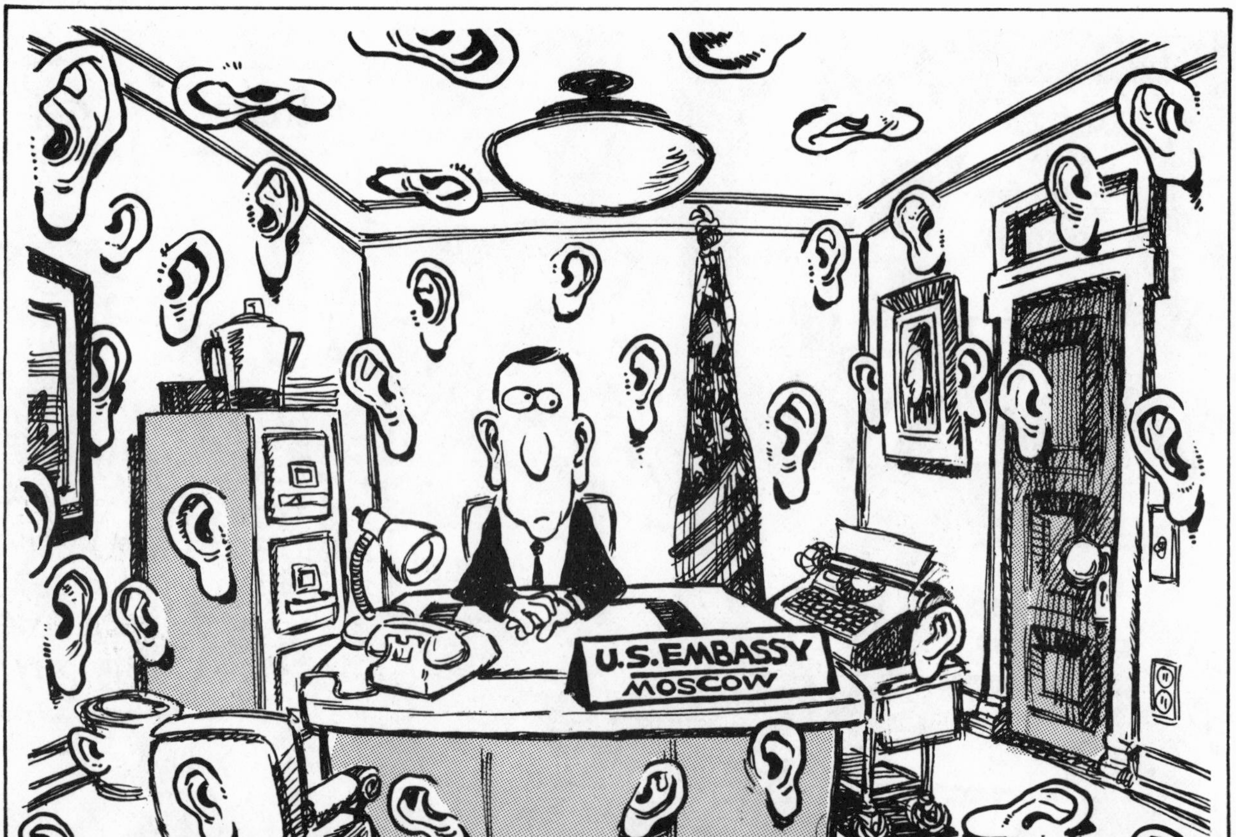
U.S. EMBASSY
MOSCOW
SACK

STEVE SACK
Courtesy Minneapolis Star-Tribune

The Stock Market

On "Black Monday," October 19, the stock market experienced a worse crash than the 1929 crash that shook the U.S. and the world. The market went into a free fall as the Dow-Jones Industrial Average declined 508 points—a whopping 22.6 percent of its value. It was the worst percentage drop since World War I, and the 604.3 million shares traded nearly doubled the old record of 338.5 million set just three days earlier.

In August, the stock market had soared to record highs, but the falling dollar—and resulting higher prices for imports—had stirred up fears of inflation. Interest rates began to move up in response to those fears.

The U.S. economy experienced its fifth consecutive year of expansion in 1987, making the economic recovery of the 1980s the second longest since World War II. But two big problems were causing real concern for the U.S.—a whopping federal budget deficit and a huge trade imbalance. These were certainly two major contributors to the crash of 1987.

DANA SUMMERS
Courtesy Orlando Sentinel

C. S. WELLS
Courtesy Augusta Chronicle

STEVE LINDSTROM
Courtesy News-Tribune & Herald (Minn.)

PIT BULL MARKET

KIRK WALTERS
Courtesy Toledo Blade

©1987 THE BLADE-TOLEDO,OH KIRK

ROGER HARVELL
Courtesy Greenville News-Piedmont

Hunger In America

DENNIS RENAULT
Courtesy Sacramento Bee

JOSEPH SZABO
© Rothco

"WELL, AT LEAST LUNCH AT THE CLUB NOW DOESN'T REQUIRE A RESERVATION!"

M. R. TINGLEY
Courtesy London (Ont.) Free Press

When the chute snaps open--!

CHUCK WERNER
Courtesy Indianapolis Star

ADRIAN RAESIDE
Courtesy Victoria (B.C.) Times-Colonist

79

ED STEIN
Courtesy Rocky Mountain News

HUGH HAYNIE
Courtesy Louisville Courier-Journal

EDD ULUSCHAK
©Southam Syndicate

TOM MEYER
Courtesy San Francisco Chronicle

MIKE GRASTON
Courtesy Windsor (Ontario) Star

AISLIN
Courtesy Montreal Gazette

GLENN FODEN
©Patuxent Publishing

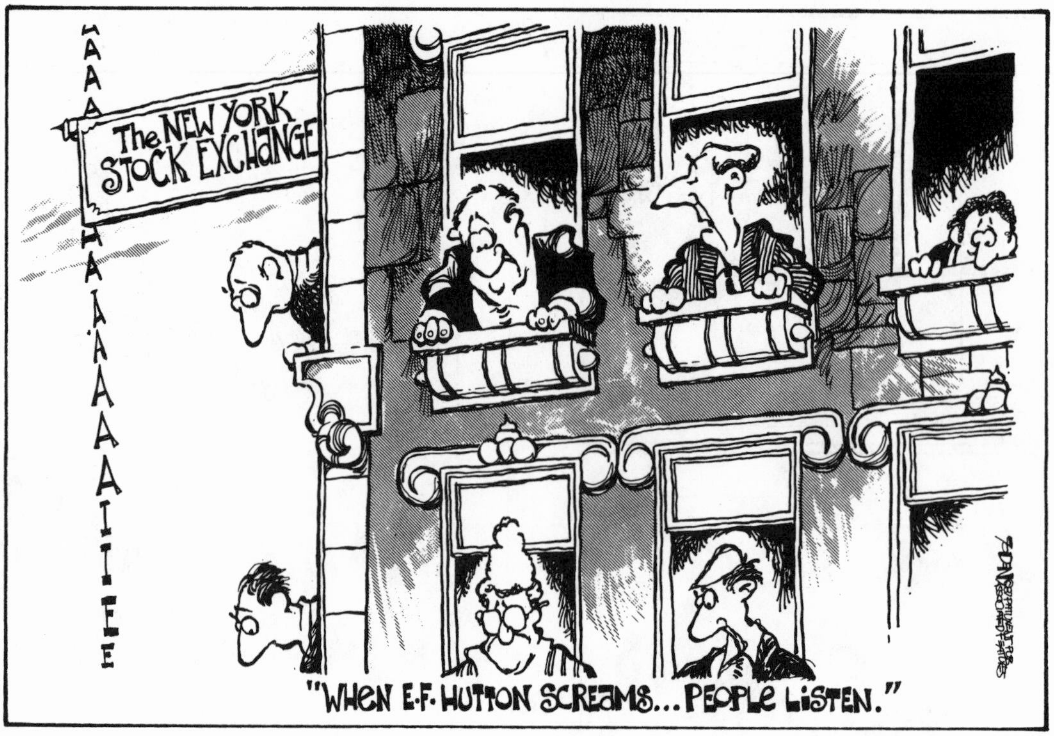
The NEW YORK STOCK EXCHANGE
"WHEN E.F. HUTTON SCREAMS... PEOPLE LISTEN."

DAVID HITCH
Courtesy Papillion (Neb.) Times

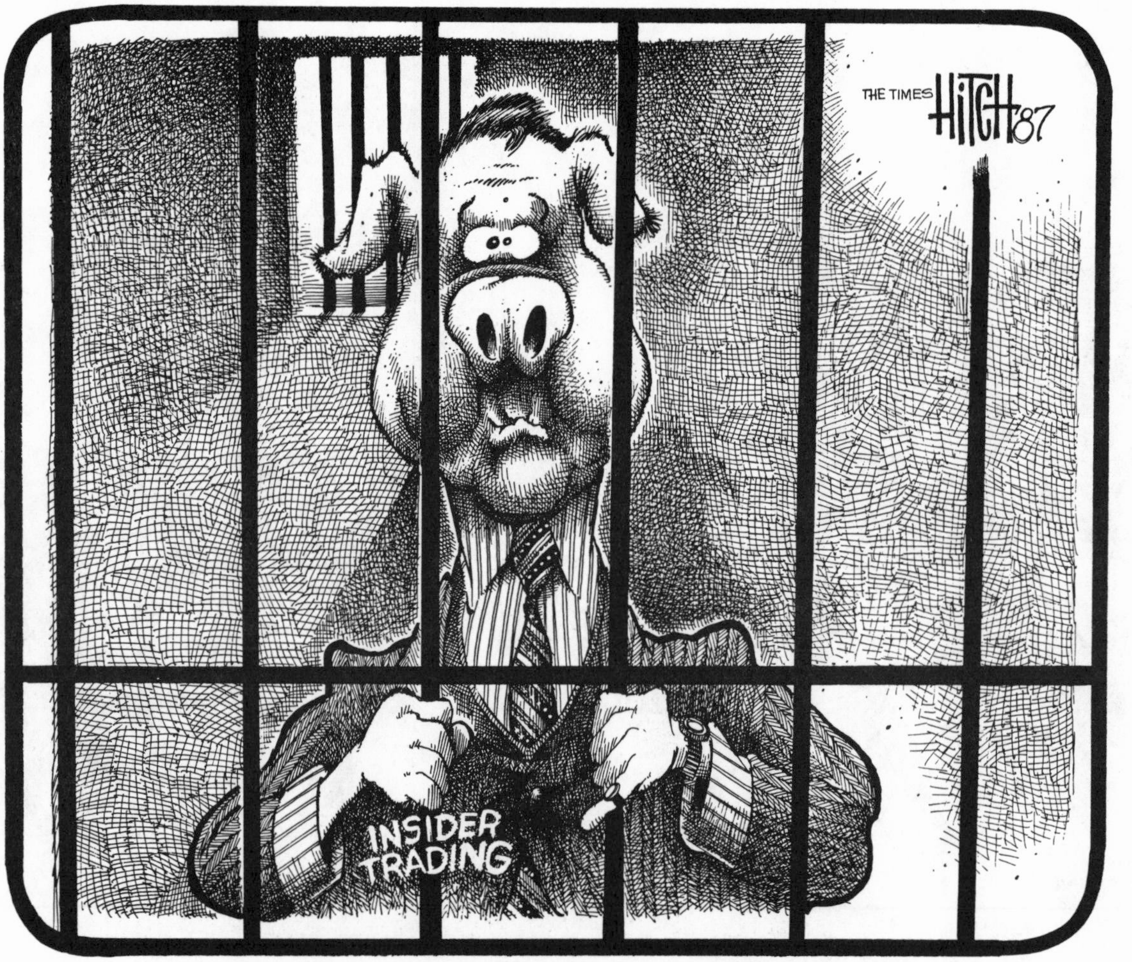
THE TIMES HITCH 87
INSIDER TRADING

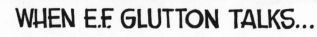

WHEN E.F. GLUTTON TALKS...

STUART CARLSON
Courtesy Milwaukee Sentinel

BILL SANDERS
Courtesy Milwaukee Journal

LINDA BOILEAU
Courtesy Frankfort State Journal

AL LIEDERMAN
© Rothco

MIKE LUCKOVICH
Courtesy Times-Picayune (New Orleans)

84

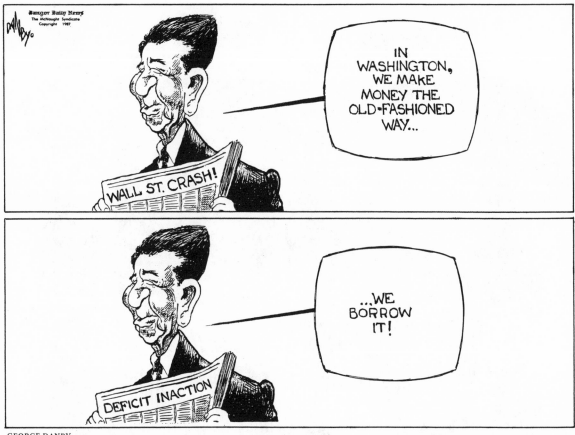

GEORGE DANBY
Courtesy Bangor Daily News

JERRY BYRD
Courtesy Beaumont Enterprise

"One World"

TOM FLANNERY
Courtesy Baltimore Sun

BRUCE BEATTIE
Courtesy Daytona Beach News-Journal

World Trade

The Reagan Administration began applying pressure on U.S. trading partners—especially Japan—during 1987 in an attempt to reverse a growing trade deficit. For much of the year the deficit continued to run at about the pace of 1986 when America imported $169.8 billion more in goods than it exported.

It was thought that the decline of the dollar would help turn the deficit around, but little immediate effect was seen. Many foreign countries cut prices and profits in order to retain their share of the U.S. market. As the year ended, the monthly deficit had fallen slightly, but everyone agreed it was still far too high.

Both houses of Congress passed tougher trade laws aimed primarily at Japan. The U.S. also was concerned about West German trade policies, and under pressure from Washington and other governments the West Germans lowered some interest rates.

World trade rose at a 3.25 percent annual rate in 1987—and predictions pointed to a 4.5 percent increase in 1988.

JOHN TREVER
Courtesy Albuquerque Journal

RICH TENNANT
© Computer World

BRUCE PLANTE
Courtesy Chattanooga Times

ART WOOD
© Farm Bureau News

DICK LOCHER
Courtesy Chicago Tribune

TV Evangelists

In the early years of television, evangelists accounted for only about two and one-half hours of programming in the typical market area. Today, however, they are beamed by more than 220 stations airing some 60 syndicated programs in a $2 billion a year industry.

In 1974 evangelist Jim Bakker founded an organization called PTL (Praise the Lord, or People That Love), which by 1986 was generating some $129 million. By March of 1987 the empire controlled by Bakker and his wife Tammy began to crumble. It was disclosed that Tammy was undergoing treatment for drugs. Then Bakker resigned from PTL after admitting that he had committed adultery with church secretary Jessica Hahn.

Bakker turned the ministry over to the fellow evangelist Jerry Falwell amid charges of gross financial mismanagement. An examination of PTL's financial records revealed that some $92 million in revenues could not be accounted for and that the ministry was $67 million in debt.

Oral Roberts made headlines in 1987 when he announced he had been told by God that if he did not raise $8 million by March 31 he would be "called home." The money was raised before the deadline. Pat Robertson, another television evangelist, announced his candidacy for the Republican presidential nomination and said he had 3.3 million petition signatures supporting his campaign.

JACK HIGGINS
Courtesy Chicago Sun-Times

FINANCIAL BANKRUPTCY

MORAL BANKRUPTCY

DER
THE GREENVILLE NEWS
LAMBERT DER
Courtesy Greenville News

VIC HARVILLE
Courtesy Texarkana Gazette

S. C. RAWLS
©NEA

DAVID HITCH
Courtesy Papillion (Neb.) Times

The Tower of Babble...

JEFF STAHLER
Courtesy Cincinnati Post

DENNIS RENAULT
Courtesy Sacramento Bee

Hands Across America

PAUL SZEP
Courtesy Boston Globe

M. R. TINGLEY
Courtesy London (Ont.) Free Press

STEVE HILL
Courtesy Oklahoma Gazette

C. S. WELLS
Courtesy Augusta Chronicle

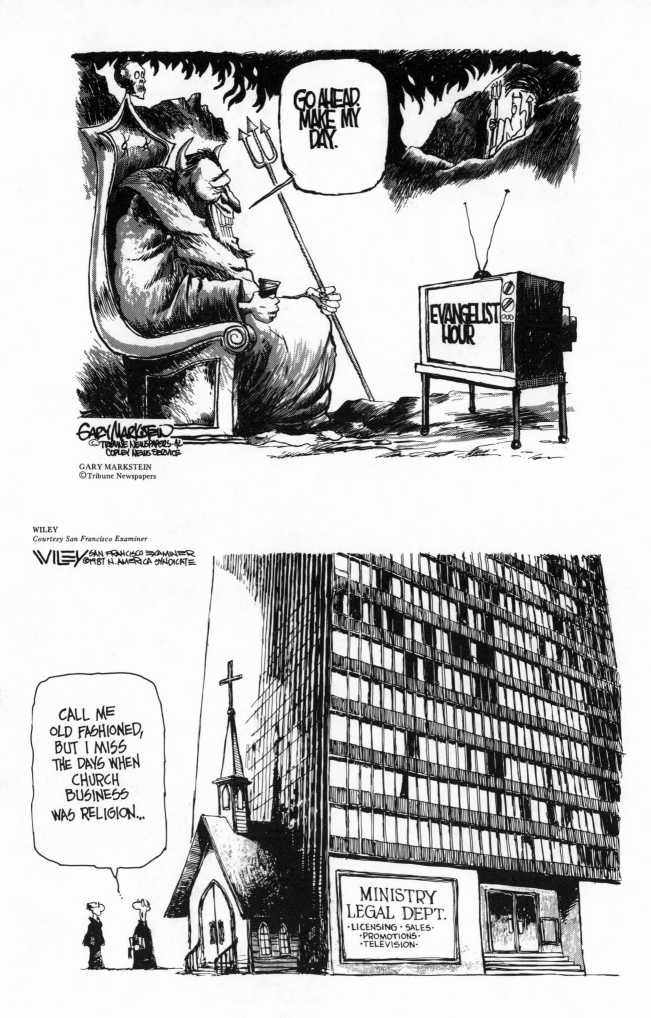

GARY MARKSTEIN
©Tribune Newspapers

WILEY
Courtesy San Francisco Examiner

TOM DARCY
©Newsday

DICK LOCHER
Courtesy Chicago Tribune

The Supreme Court

President Reagan was handed an opportunity to try to tilt the Supreme Court's ideological balance when Justice Lewis Powell retired unexpectedly in June. Powell had often been the swing vote in the court's 5 to 4 decisions. Reagan nominated a conservative U.S. appeals court judge, Robert Bork, who had been a Yale University law professor.

A lobbying campaign against Bork was immediately launched by liberal Democrats in Congress and various other pressure groups. Sen. Ted Kennedy and Sen. Joseph Biden, chairman of the Senate Judiciary Committee which was investigating Bork's qualifications, led the drive to defeat the nomination. Reagan and Bork carried the fight to the Senate floor where the nomination was rejected by a 58 to 42 vote. The issue clearly had been decided on the basis of politics, not the nominee's qualifications.

The President then nominated another conservative, Douglas H. Ginsburg, who had been a Harvard Law School professor. Ginsburg was forced to withdraw from consideration, however, after admitting he had used marijuana several times while in college.

Reagan finally submitted the name of another appeals court judge, Anthony Kennedy. He was considered to be less conservative than Bork or Ginsburg, and was expected to be confirmed.

GENE BASSET
Courtesy Atlanta Journal

"THE PRESIDENT MAY PRESENT HIS NOMINEE TO REPLACE JUSTICE POWELL."

CHUCK ASAY
Courtesy Colorado Springs Gazette

BOB SULLIVAN
Courtesy Worcester (Mass.) Telegram

ROGER HARVELL
Courtesy Greenville News-Piedmont

GEORGE DANBY
Courtesy Bangor Daily News

JERRY BARNETT
Courtesy Indianapolis News

DRAPER HILL
Courtesy Detroit News

JOHN TREVER
Courtesy Albuquerque Journal

"...THEN THE BIG, BAD BORK HUFFED AND HE PUFFED AND HE BLEW THE
CONSTITUTION DOWN, AND HE GOBBLED UP ALL THE WOMEN AND MINORITIES!..."

MIKE SHELTON
Courtesy Orange County Register

BOB RICH
Courtesy New Haven Register

BRIAN BASSET
Courtesy Seattle Times

"Hang in there, Bob."

TOM FLOYD
Courtesy Gary Post-Tribune

DAVID CATROW
Courtesy Springfield (Oh.) News-Sun

THE CHIEF JUSTICE OF THE U.S. SUPREME COURT ADMINISTERS THE PRESIDENTIAL OATH OF OFFICE TO C.R.(STINKY) MILLER—

CHARLES DANIEL
Courtesy Knoxville Journal

ED GAMBLE
Courtesy Florida Times-Union

CHUCK WERNER
Courtesy Indianapolis Star

JOHN BRANCH
Courtesy San Antonio Express-News

JERRY BUCKLEY
Courtesy Montgomery Spirit

STEVE HILL
Courtesy Oklahoma Gazette

S. C. RAWLS
©NEA

BOB GORRELL
Courtesy Richmond News Leader

104

LOUIS (DOC) GOODWIN
Courtesy Columbus Dispatch

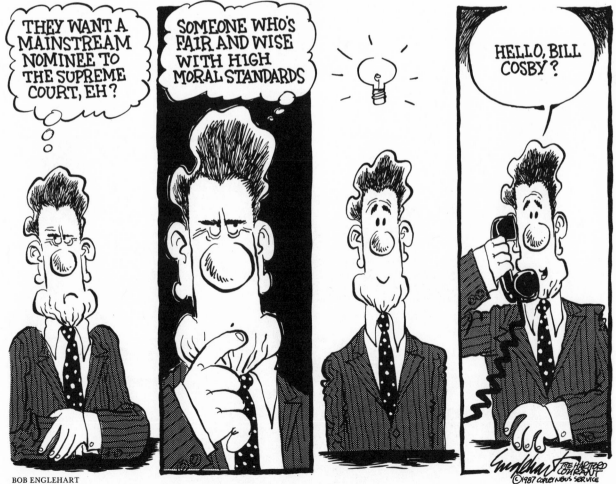

BOB ENGLEHART
Courtesy Hartford Courant

The Economy

The U.S. economy continued to expand well into 1987, making the economic recovery of the 1980s the second longest since World War II. During the first half of the year, economists expressed considerable optimism about continued growth. But by the third quarter, rising interest rates and signs of renewed inflation began to create concern.

America's two troubling deficits—in the federal budget and in international trade—formed a black cloud over a jittery business world. The federal deficit, which for 1986 reached $220.7 billion, was trimmed to $148 billion for 1987. But it remained far too high, and was the source of continuing concern. The trade deficit stood at $169.8 billion in 1986 and was expected to top that figure for 1987.

The dollar plummeted some 40 percent against other major currencies and by November was trading at postwar record lows against the Japanese yen and the German mark.

Texaco was found by a Texas court to have illegally interfered with a merger agreement between the Getty Oil Company and Pennzoil. Pennzoil was awarded a staggering $10.53 billion in damages, but Texaco announced it would ask the U.S. Supreme Court to review the case.

A Van Gogh painting, "Sunflowers," was sold for a record $39.9 million to a Japanese company in March, and later in the year another Van Gogh, "Irises," brought $53.9 million.

ROB ROGERS
Courtesy Pittsburgh Press

MARTIN GARRITY
Courtesy Fair Oaks (Calif.) Post

DAVID KOLOSTA
Courtesy Houston Post

CLAY BENNETT
Courtesy St. Petersburg Times

DON LANDGREN
Courtesy The (Mass.) Landmark

EDDIE GERMANO
Courtesy Brockton Enterprise

CLAY BENNETT
Courtesy St. Petersburg Times

JOHN CRAWFORD
Courtesy Alabama Journal

ROB ROGERS
Courtesy Pittsburgh Press

The Congress

For the first time since 1980, the Democrats in 1987 found themselves in control of both houses of Congress. Sen. Robert C. Byrd (D-W.Va.) became the new Senate majority leader, and Rep. Jim Wright (D-Tex.) took over as House speaker.

Congress was unable to deal with the huge federal deficit despite heated debates during the year. When the stock market crashed on October 19, however, congressional leaders finally were compelled to come to grips with the problem. Their proposed solution included tax increases and spending cuts that would lower the deficit by at least $23 billion. The Democrats had long favored higher taxes, while President Reagan had steadfastly opposed them. Congress apparently made no effort to follow the Gramm-Rudman guidelines in constructing their proposal.

House Speaker Jim Wright found himself in the eye of the hurricane in November when he met with Nicaraguan leader Daniel Ortega. He was accused by President Reagan, as well as by other congressmen and newspapers around the country, of attempting to conduct his own foreign policy. Wright even issued an 11-point plan intended, in his words, to be the blueprint for cease-fire talks with the Contras. Wright used various forums to try to advance his own ideas of foreign policy—which often were at odds with official U.S. policy.

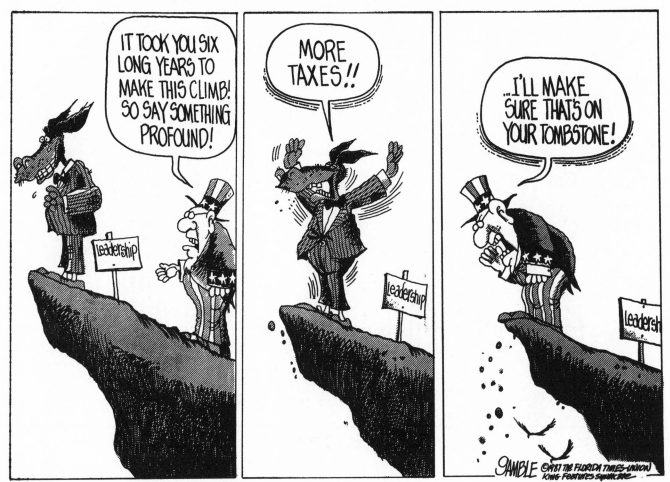

ED GAMBLE
Courtesy Florida Times-Union

LEFT WAITING AT THE CHURCH AGAIN

ART WOOD
© Farm Bureau News

ED GAMBLE
Courtesy Florida Times-Union

MICHAEL RAMIREZ
© Baker Communications

HANK WILSON
Courtesy Baton Rouge State-Times

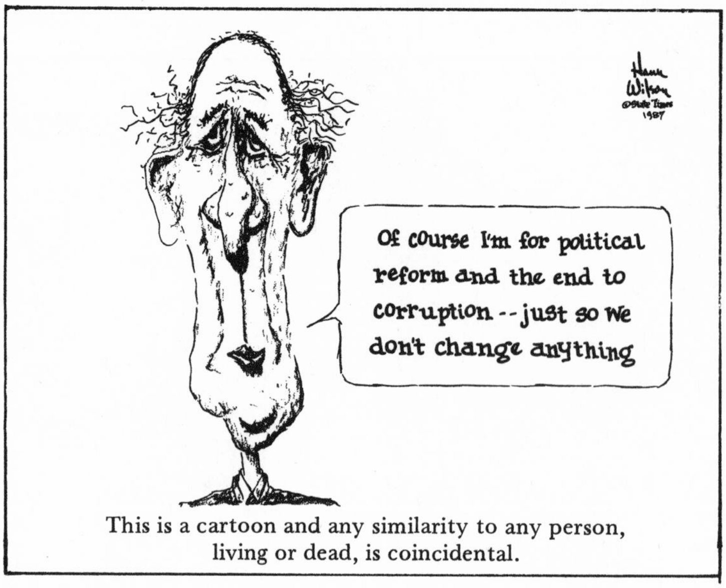
Hank Wilson ©State-Times 1987
Of course I'm for political reform and the end to corruption -- just so we don't change anything
This is a cartoon and any similarity to any person, living or dead, is coincidental.

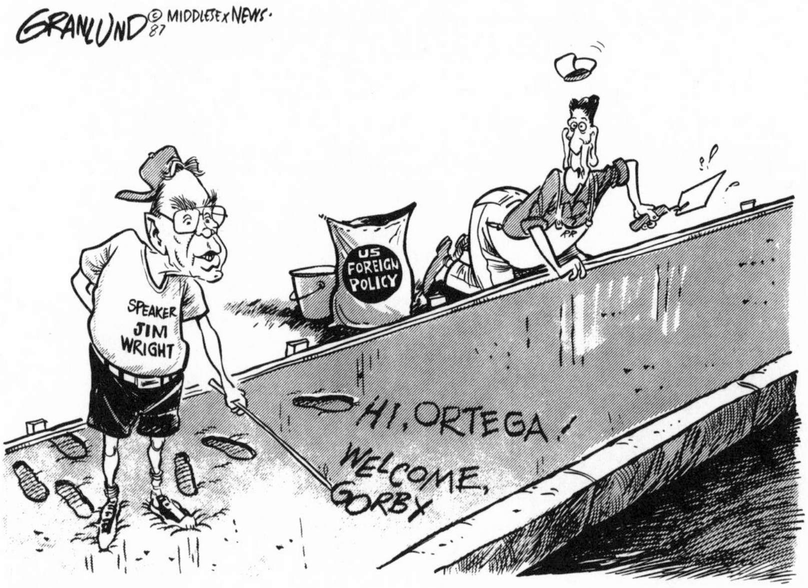
GRANLUND © 87 MIDDLESEX NEWS
US FOREIGN POLICY
SPEAKER JIM WRIGHT
HI, ORTEGA!
WELCOME, GORBY

DAVE GRANLUND
Courtesy Middlesex (Mass.) News

DICK WRIGHT
Courtesy Providence Journal-Bulletin

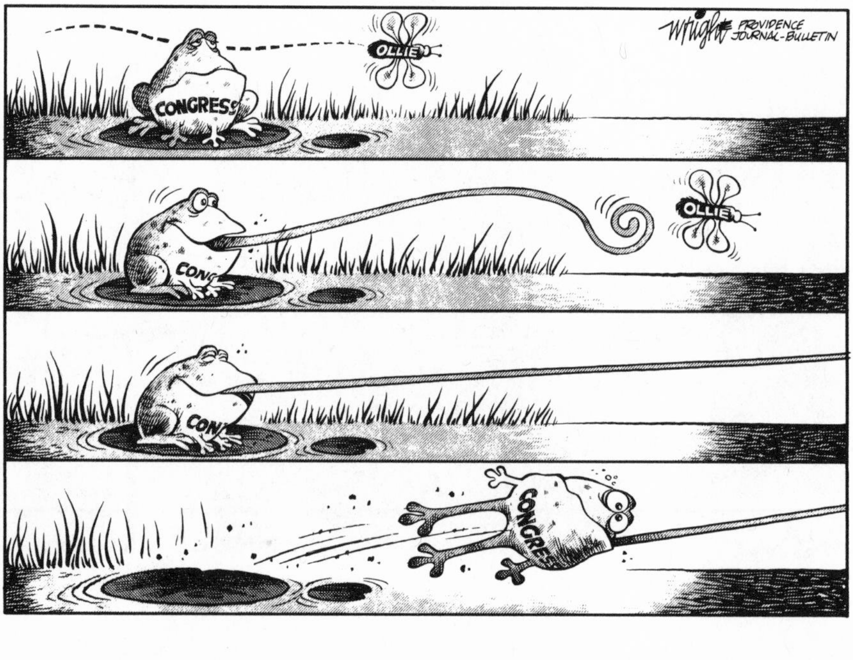
Wright PROVIDENCE JOURNAL-BULLETIN
CONGRESS
OLLIE
CONG
OLLIE
CON
CONGRESS

STEVE MC BRIDE
Courtesy Independence (Kan.) Daily Reporter

ELDON PLETCHER
© Rothco

GENE BASSET
Courtesy Atlanta Journal

The Papal Visit

During the nine years John Paul II has been pope, he has drastically changed the conduct of the papacy. He has traveled over 334,000 miles and has become a highly visible pontiff. Although he is a social liberal, he is strongly conservative in church doctrine.

As the pope crossed the U.S. in 1987, visiting nine cities, he repeatedly stressed that a good Catholic must adhere to all church teachings. It is not enough, he said, to follow some and ignore others.

One startling decision John Paul II made was to receive Austrian President Kurt Waldheim on an official visit to the Vatican in June. Waldheim is facing growing accusations of deep involvement in Nazi atrocities during World War II. Jewish people were upset, and many Catholics expressed concern as well.

John Paul II also made visits in 1987 to Chile, Poland, Argentina, Uruguay, and Canada. He urged Poles to assert themselves in pursuit of liberty and challenged Communist governments to respect human rights.

LARRY WRIGHT
Courtesy Detroit News

J. D. CROWE
Courtesy San Diego Tribune

JAMES TODD
©Southam Syndicate

STEVE MC BRIDE
Courtesy Independence (Kan.) Daily Reporter

JOHN KNUDSEN
Courtesy The Tidings

CHAN LOWE
Courtesy News/Sun-Sentinel (Fort Lauderdale)

STEVE KELLY
Courtesy San Diego Union

Health Issues

U.S. Surgeon General C. Everett Koop, in his yearly report on smoking and health, warned that breathing near people with lighted cigarettes in enclosed areas can cause lung cancer in nonsmokers. He also pointed out that children of parents who smoke are more likely to have respiratory infections than children of nonsmokers.

More and more cities across the country enacted ordinances curbing smoking in public buildings and on public carriers. And the tobacco industry came out with what is claimed to be a smokeless cigarette.

During the year, the Environmental Protection Agency added 99 hazardous waste sites to the list of locations eligible for federal clean-up, making a total of 802 sites. The EPA also prohibited land disposal of 12 different classes of hazardous waste.

President Reagan and Canada's Prime Minister Brian Mulroney agreed in April to consider a bilateral solution to the acid-rain problem. The U.S. agreed to spend $2.35 billion over five years on the development of clean coal-burning technologies.

ART HENRIKSON
© Paddock Publications, Inc.

SMOKELESS CIGARETTE DEVELOPED BY R.J. REYNOLDS TOBACCO CO.

• AN AMERICAN HOSTAGE •

FIRST THE GOOD NEWS . . .

118

'Nice and leisurely...a slow, easy taste. The pleasure lasts
and lasts. Some things you just can't hurry.' — Cigarette Ad

AL LIEDERMAN
© Rothco

WAYNE STAYSKAL
Courtesy Tampa Tribune

RAOUL HUNTER
Courtesy Le Soleil

JIM BORGMAN
Courtesy Cincinnati Enquirer

"THIS IS GREAT! NOW WHEN I GET TIRED OF WORRYING ABOUT NUCLEAR DESTRUCTION, I CAN WORRY ABOUT THE THREAT OF MASS OBLITERATION RIGHT HERE ON OUR OWN INTERSTATE!"

BRIAN DUFFY
Courtesy Des Moines Register

AIDS

Controversy raged during the year over AIDS (Acquired Immune Deficiency Syndrome): How great the threat? How best to treat it? What screening programs are needed to slow the spread of the disease? How helpful are general education programs promoting "safe sex"? When, if ever, will an effective vaccine be available?

At the end of 1987, more than 46,000 cases of AIDS had been reported in the U.S., and some 26,000 of the victims had died. Health officials have predicted that by 1992, AIDS cases in the U.S. could total 270,000, with as many as 170,000 deaths.

Although 95 percent of all cases in America have occurred among intravenous drug users or homosexual men, there was growing concern of an apparent increase in the spread of the disease by heterosexuals. Dr. C. Everett Koop, surgeon-general of the U.S., spoke out strongly on the subject, urging early sex education in the schools and the use of television advertisements for condoms in an attempt to halt the spread of the deadly disease.

STEVE KELLY
Courtesy San Diego Union

TOM MEYER
Courtesy San Francisco Chronicle

JOHN BRANCH
Courtesy San Antonio Express-News

RAY OSRIN
Courtesy Cleveland Plain Dealer

BOB ENGLEHART
Courtesy Hartford Courant

MILT PRIGGEE
Courtesy Spokane Chronicle

SUE DEWAR
Courtesy Calgary Sun

JOHN CRAWFORD
Courtesy Alabama Journal

125

KEN ALEXANDER
©Copley News Service

MIKE LUCKOVICH
Courtesy Times-Picayune (New Orleans)

BOB DORNFRIED
© Rothco

BILL SANDERS
Courtesy Milwaukee Journal

"Hey, soldier, remember that peace slogan the kids used to shout — 'Make love, not war'?"

TOM DARCY
© Newsday

ED STEIN
Courtesy Rocky Mountain News

WAYNE STAYSKAL
Courtesy Tampa Tribune

"TWO TO ONE HE STAYS IN AGAIN TONIGHT!"

Air Travel

The U.S. airline industry enjoyed a record year in 1986, transporting some 418 million passengers, and for 1987 the number was estimated to have soared to 450 million. The rising number of travelers, however, seemed to be overwhelming the airline industry and airports around the country. Consumers became more and more irate over misplaced baggage, overbooked flights, flight delays, and congestion in the skies. There also were scores of documented cases of near-collisions and other odd incidents as air traffic continued to grow. The burden on air traffic controllers was heavy, and often control centers were understaffed.

One of the nation's worst crashes ever occurred in Detroit on August 16 when a Northwest Airlines jet crashed just after takeoff, killing 156 people.

Deregulation was cited by many observers as the major cause of many of the industry's problems. They insisted it has allowed too much traffic to clog the airways. Others blame the "hub-and-spoke" system, which feeds travelers into a few major airports. At peak departure and arrival times, terminal facilities and traffic control can become overloaded. Still another problem to surface during the year was the alleged use of drugs among airline personnel.

DICK LOCHER
Courtesy Chicago Tribune

DAN WASSERMAN
Courtesy Boston Globe

PHIL BISSELL
Courtesy Lowell Sun

CHAN LOWE
Courtesy News/Sun-Sentinel (Fort Lauderdale)

ALAN KING
Courtesy Ottawa Citizen

ITS CUP RUNNETH OVER

EDDIE GERMANO
Courtesy Brockton Enterprise

STEVE KELLY
Courtesy San Diego Union

131

BUBBA FLINT
Courtesy Dallas/Ft. Worth Suburban Newspaper

LOUIS (DOC) GOODWIN
Courtesy Columbus Dispatch

The American Family

Worldwide, 500 children have been born to surrogate mothers since 1978. About 25 surrogate centers are now operating in the U.S., matching interested couples with surrogates. Their services include medical and psychological screening of participants and the drafting of agreements between interested parties.

This has created unusual relationships and unique problems that did not exist before. Some surrogates are paid, while others are not. Some see it as a chance to bring real happiness to infertile couples. But, under the laws of most states, the surrogate is recognized as the legal mother at the time of birth.

In such arrangements, the social relationships, legal rights, and responsibilities of the various parties will have to be decided by the courts and lawmakers of the land.

DAVID HORSEY
Courtesy Seattle Post-Intelligencer

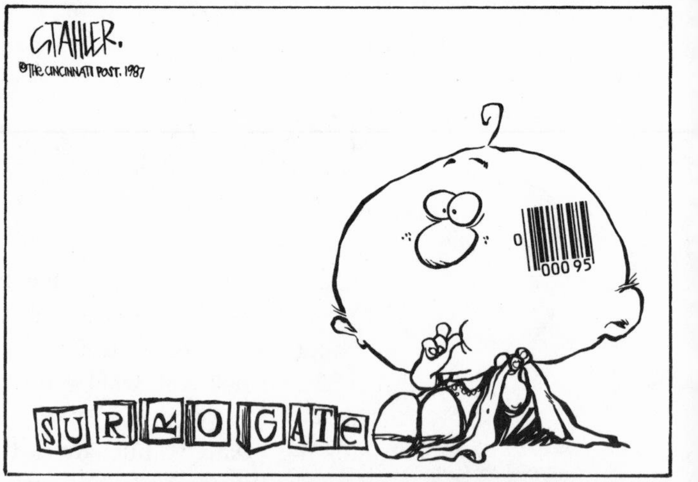
STAHLER.
© THE CINCINNATI POST, 1987
000 95
SURROGATE

JEFF STAHLER
Courtesy Cincinnati Post

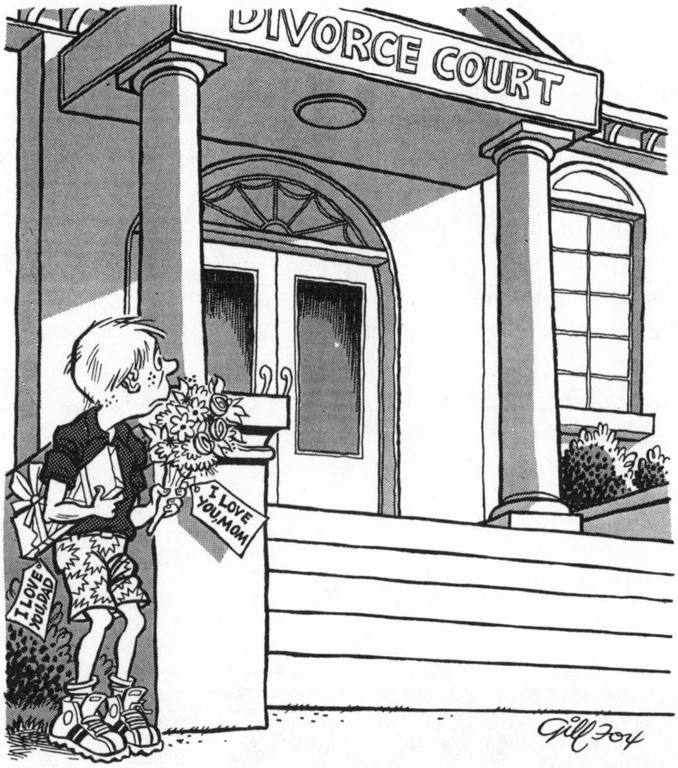
DIVORCE COURT
I LOVE YOU, MOM
I LOVE YOU, DAD
Gill Fox

GILL FOX
Courtesy Greenwich News

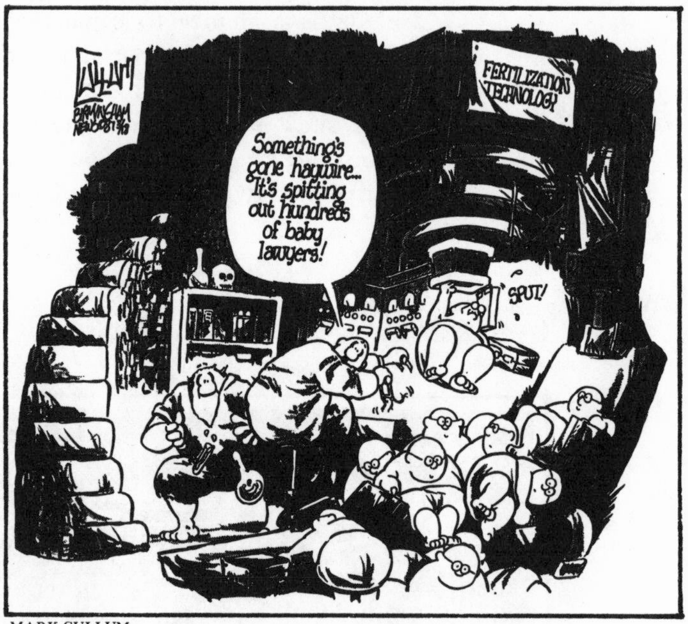
CULLUM
BIRMINGHAM NEWS
FERTILIZATION TECHNOLOGY
Something's gone haywire... It's spitting out hundreds of baby lawyers!
SPUT!

MARK CULLUM
Courtesy Birmingham News

CHARLES DANIEL
Courtesy Knoxville Journal

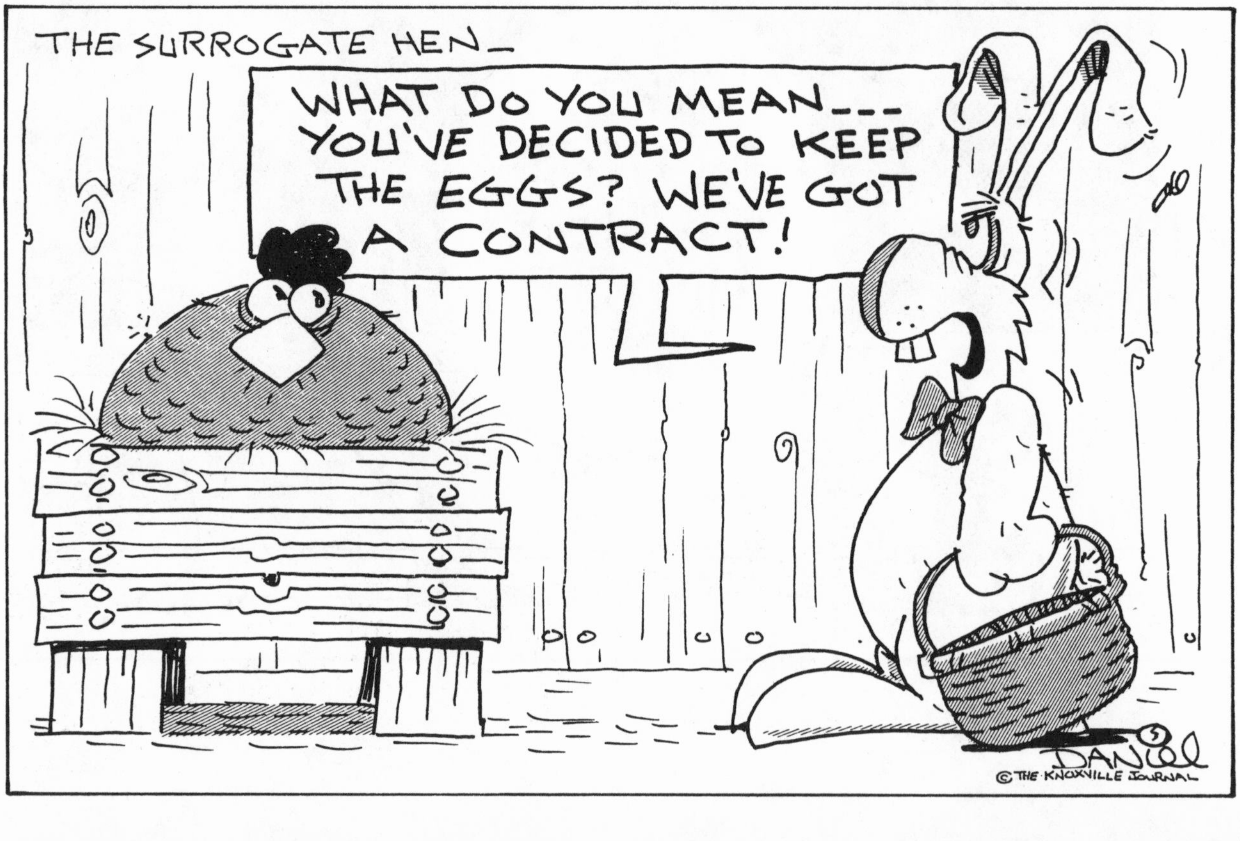
THE SURROGATE HEN_
WHAT DO YOU MEAN___ YOU'VE DECIDED TO KEEP THE EGGS? WE'VE GOT A CONTRACT!
DANIEL
© THE KNOXVILLE JOURNAL

AMERICAN PROFILE:

This is Betty Jo Hepplewaite.

You probably never heard of her.

She is religious, but doesn't shove her beliefs down the throats of others.

She has never run for office or marched in protest.

She votes on every election day.

She has never sued anyone or ever been sued.

She has never written a book about her criminal life because she's never had one.

She's never had a one night stand with an evangelist, shredded documents for the White House, or discussed her sexual preference on "Donahue".

She has never checked into the Betty Ford clinic.

There are no nude photos of her in Playboy's files.

Betty Jo Hepplewaite is simply a decent, law abiding, hard working American

...which may explain why you never heard of her.

WILEY
Courtesy San Francisco Examiner

FASCISM'S ATROCITY

AUSCHWITZ

COMMUNISM'S ATROCITY

SIBERIAN PRISON No. 13

DEMOCRACY'S ATROCITY

WEST SIDE ABORTION CLINIC

LOU BLOSS
Courtesy Alexandria Daily Town Talk

The Constitution

Citizens throughout America celebrated the 200th anniversary of the U.S. Constitution in 1987. Many cities held observances, but the biggest took place in Philadelphia where the Constitution was drafted.

In September, President Reagan spoke at a nationally televised affair called "We the People 200." Participants included descendants of the original 39 signers of the Constitution.

The U.S. Mint issued two unusual commemorative coins to mark the 200th anniversary celebration, and the U.S. Postal Service published a five-stamp booklet featuring quotations from the preamble of the Constitution. Single stamps featuring the 1787 signing ceremony also were issued.

MIKE LUCKOVICH
Courtesy Times-Picayune (New Orleans)

BERT WHITMAN
Courtesy Phoenix Gazette

HUGH HAYNIE
Courtesy Louisville Courier-Journal

BILL MITCHELL
©Gannett Rochester Newspapers

Canadian Affairs

The Mulroney government's biggest issue during 1987 was the matter of free trade. When talks with President Reagan were begun in 1986, free trade had been the major issue the Canadians wanted resolved. To Canadians, the issue was tied directly to the matter of national identity. Many Canadians feel that their country is completely overshadowed in trade relations by their more powerful neighbor to the south.

A tentative agreement was announced in October that included gradual abolition of cross-border tariffs by January 1, 1999, a panel to hear appeals against countervailing duties, reduction of barriers to energy imports and exports, and the opening of government procurement for companies in both countries.

Many Canadians were highly critical of the agreement, however, labeling it a sellout of Canadian economic independence. Late in 1987, the Reagan Administration announced further concessions on the issue.

Acid rain continued as a topic of major concern as Canada sought to force more of the factories and plants in the northeastern U.S. to cease discharging toxic wastes into the atmosphere.

JAMES TODD
©Southam Syndicate

EDD ULUSCHAK
©Southam Syndicate

"DIDN'T YOU GET OUR NOTICE?"

ADRIAN RAESIDE
Courtesy Victoria (B.C.) Times-Colonist

MIKE GRASTON
Courtesy Windsor (Ontario) Star

139

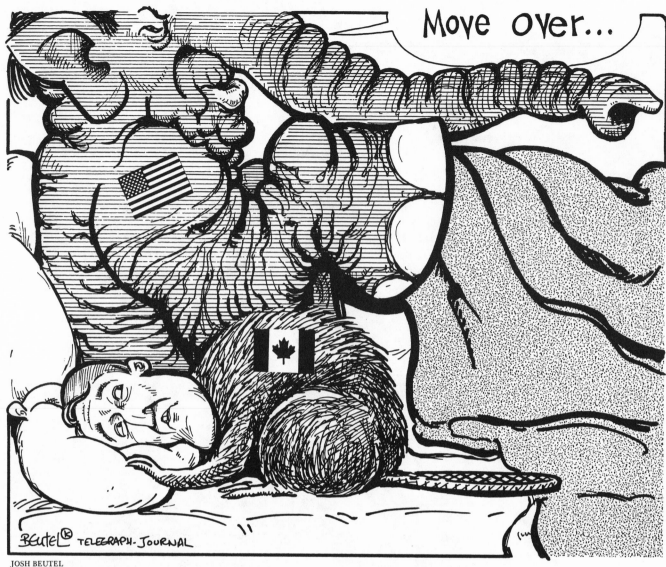

JOSH BEUTEL
Courtesy Telegraph-Journal (Canada)

M. R. TINGLEY
Courtesy London (Ont.) Free Press

ADRIAN RAESIDE
Courtesy Victoria (B.C.) Times-Colonist

Sports

After several weeks of negotiations on a new contract, National Football League players walked out on September 22. It was the fifth strike for the NFL since 1974.

The main issue was a demand by the players for unrestricted free agency. This would mean that once a player's contract had expired, he would be free to sign with another team—with no compensation being given to his old team.

The owners were adamantly opposed to the proposal and refused to budge an inch. The players contended that the collective-bargaining agreement they had been working under was unfair to the players because the compensation required was so high that it effectively killed free agency.

One week of play was canceled, and the teams resumed the schedule, playing three games with replacement teams. It was October 25 before the strike was completely over and normal games, with regulars, resumed.

The generally accepted verdict on the outcome of the strike was Owners 1, Players 0.

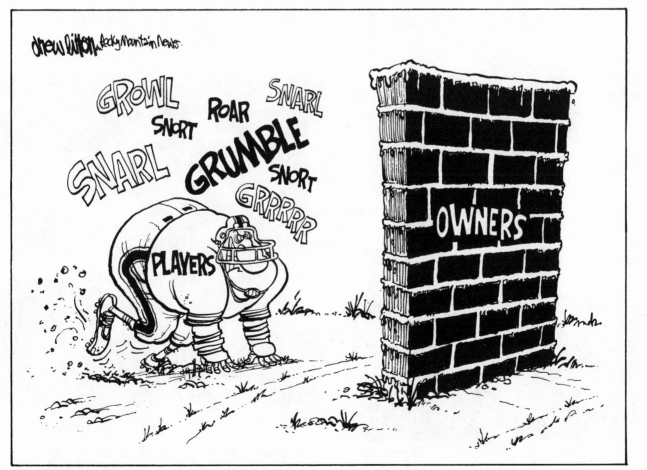

DREW LITTON
Courtesy Rocky Mountain News

"BELIEVE ME, KID, NOBODY WANTS A STRIKE. BUT WE'VE GOT PAYMENTS TO MAKE ON THE CONDO, THE PORSHE, THE JAG, AND THE SAILBOAT... JUST LIKE EVERYONE ELSE."

"C'MON GIRLS... LET'S PRACTICE THAT ROUTINE AGAIN... YOU NEVER KNOW WHEN THOSE NFL CHEERLEADERS WILL GO ON STRIKE..."

"WELCOME TO THE NFL, KID."

C. S. WELLS
Courtesy Augusta Chronicle

CHUCK ASAY
Courtesy Colorado Springs Gazette

PAUL FELL
Courtesy Lincoln Journal

DREW LITTON
Courtesy Rocky Mountain News

144   DAVID HORSEY
Courtesy Seattle Post-Intelligencer

DREW LITTON
Courtesy Rocky Mountain News

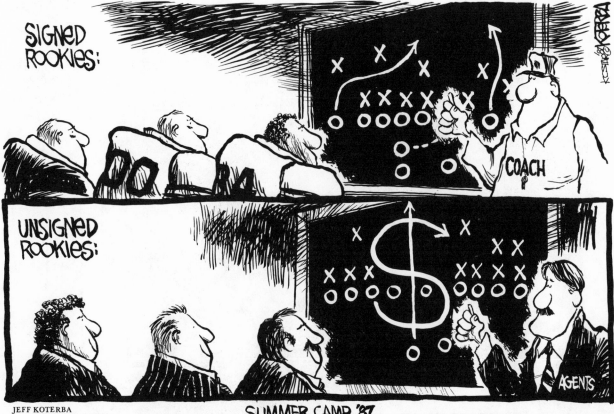

JEFF KOTERBA
Courtesy Kansas City Star

145

. . . And Other Issues

A major scandal erupted in 1987 when two U.S. Marine guards at the U.S. embassy in Moscow were accused of allowing Russian agents into sensitive areas of the embassy in exchange for sexual favors. Charges were later dropped against one of the Marines, but Sgt. Clayton J. Lonetree was given a 30-year prison sentence. In California, a spree of violence broke out on the Los Angeles freeways as motorists were shot at in what appeared to be frustration with the traffic. Some 120 shooting incidents were reported.

The U.S space program, in disarray after the space shuttle explosion in 1986, continued to founder. The Soviets, on the other hand, moved ahead with a record-setting MIR space station flight, the firing of a new Energia booster, and the launching of more than 100 unmanned space projects. A French group brought up from the final resting place of the *Titanic* hundreds of artifacts, including dishes, jewelry, and a chandelier. The items were placed in museums.

A garbage barge from Islip, New York, made news during the spring with its 3,100 tons of waste. The barge's crew tried unsuccessfully to unload the trash along the coasts of several states, but finally returned to Brooklyn where the waste was incinerated.

Many well-known personalities died during the year, among them Fred Astaire, Mary Astor, Jackie Gleason, Rita Hayworth, Danny Kaye, Liberace, and Clare Booth Luce.

JIM BORGMAN
Courtesy Cincinnati Enquirer

" A MISTER ASTAIRE TO SEE YOU, BOSS......"

TOM FLANNERY
Courtesy Baltimore Sun

Fred Astaire 1899-1987

BOB SULLIVAN
Courtesy Worcester (Mass.) Telegram

DOUG MAC GREGOR
Courtesy Norwich (Conn.) Bulletin

JERRY BARNETT
Courtesy Indianapolis News

JERRY FEARING
Courtesy St. Paul Pioneer Press

ALAN KING
Courtesy Ottawa Citizen

"So I've told Mary Lou she can go out with that young man just as long as he's not a preacher, a marine or a presidential candidate."

JIMMY MARGULIES
Courtesy Houston Post

"Shall we take the Marine guard on line 1... the TV evangelist on line 2... or Gary Hart on line 3 ?... "

JEFF STAHLER
Courtesy Cincinnati Post

DISCRIMINATION

JIM LANGE
Courtesy Daily Oklahoman

DANA SUMMERS
Courtesy Orlando Sentinel

BOB ENGLEHART
Courtesy Hartford Courant

"CAREFUL, COMRADES — THERE'S LIGHT
AT THE END OF THE TUNNEL!"

IT'S ABOUT TIME HESS
SHOWED UP— AFTER ALL THAT
LAVISH LIVING AT SPANDAU
FOR ALL THOSE YEARS!

VAGABOND GARBAGE SCOW

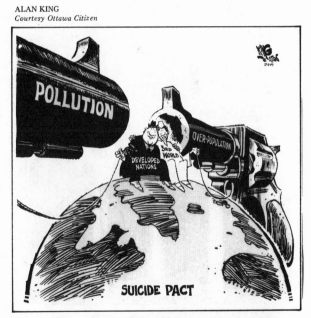

SUICIDE PACT

DAVID KOLOSTA
Courtesy Houston Post

HOUSTON POST KOLOSTA

TOM GIBB
Courtesy Altoona Mirror

"WHOOPS.   TERRIBLY SORRY."

DANI AGUILA
Courtesy Filipino Reporter

JOEL PETT
Courtesy Lexington (Ky.) Herald-Leader

CHARLES BISSELL
Courtesy The Tennessean

Window to the unknown

BOB SULLIVAN
Courtesy Worcester (Mass.) Telegram

"Dear Mrs. Jones; Your Billy always speaks out of turn and is incredibly rude, loud and drisruptive. I'm sure he'll make a fine White House correspondent some day."

PAT BAGLEY
Courtesy Salt Lake Tribune

BRUCE PLANTE
Courtesy Chattanooga Times

SPYDER WEBB
Courtesy Blade-Tribune (Calif.)

Addison ©87
THE JOURNAL
RISING HEALTH CARE COSTS
OPEN YOUR MOUTH AND SAY "AAH."

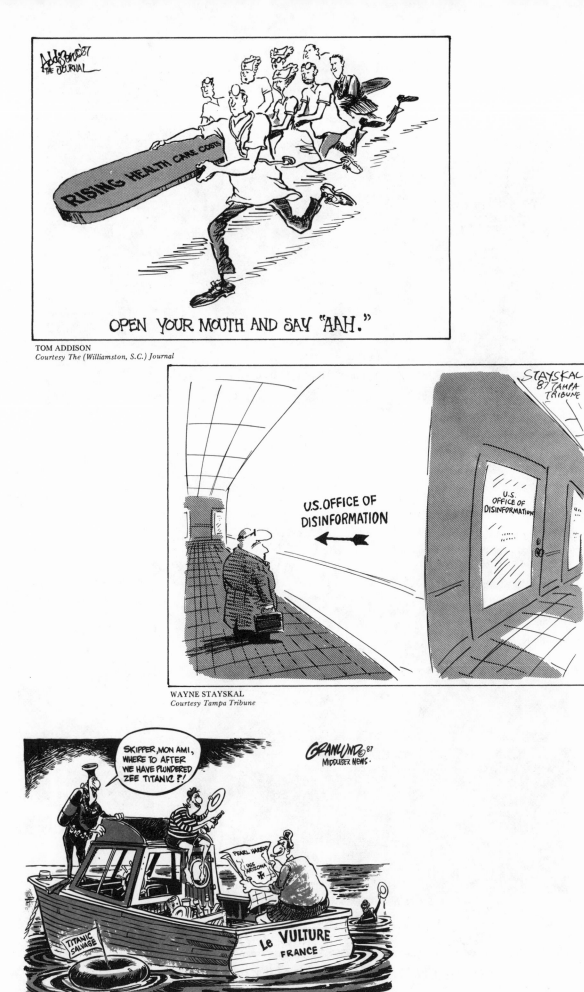

TOM ADDISON
Courtesy The (Williamston, S.C.) Journal

STAYSKAL
87 TAMPA
TRIBUNE
U.S. OFFICE OF
DISINFORMATION
U.S.
OFFICE OF
DISINFORMATION

WAYNE STAYSKAL
Courtesy Tampa Tribune

SKIPPER, MON AMI, WHERE TO AFTER WE HAVE PLUNDERED ZEE TITANIC ?!
GRANLUND ©87
MIDDLESEX NEWS.
PEARL HARBOR
USS ARIZONA
TITANIC SALVAGE
Le VULTURE
FRANCE

DAVE GRANLUND
Courtesy Middlesex (Mass.) News

CHUCK AYERS
Courtesy Akron Beacon-Journal

Jake shows off Jezebel's new litter

LEN BORO
Courtesy Phoenix Gazette

Past Award Winners

SIGMA DELTA CHI AWARD
EDITORIAL CARTOON

1942—Jacob Burck, Chicago Times
1943—Charles Werner, Chicago Sun
1944—Henry Barrow, Associated Press
1945--Reuben L. Goldberg, New York Sun
1946—Dorman H. Smith, Newspaper Enterprise Association
1947—Bruce Russell, Los Angeles Times
1948—Herbert Block, Washington Post
1949—Herbert Block, Washington Post
1950—Bruce Russell, Los Angeles Times
1951—Herbert Block, Washington Post, and
    Bruce Russell, Los Angeles Times
1952—Cecil Jensen, Chicago Daily News
1953—John Fischetti, Newspaper Enterprise Association
1954—Calvin Alley, Memphis Commercial Appeal
1955—John Fischetti, Newspaper Enterprise Association
1956—Herbert Block, Washington Post
1957—Scott Long, Minneapolis Tribune
1958—Clifford H. Baldowski, Atlanta Constitution
1959—Charles G. Brooks, Birmingham News
1960—Dan Dowling, New York Herald-Tribune
1961—Frank Interlandi, Des Moines Register
1962—Paul Conrad, Denver Post
1963—William Mauldin, Chicago Sun-Times
1964—Charles Bissell, Nashville Tennessean
1965—Roy Justus, Minneapolis Star
1966—Patrick Oliphant, Denver Post
1967—Eugene Payne, Charlotte Observer
1968—Paul Conrad, Los Angeles Times
1969—William Mauldin, Chicago Sun-Times
1970—Paul Conrad, Los Angeles Times
1971—Hugh Haynie, Louisville Courier-Journal
1972—William Mauldin, Chicago Sun-Times
1973—Paul Szep, Boston Globe
1974—Mike Peters, Dayton Daily News
1975—Tony Auth, Philadelphia Enquirer
1976—Paul Szep, Boston Globe
1977—Don Wright, Miami News
1978—Jim Borgman, Cincinnati Enquirer
1979—John P. Trever, Albuquerque Journal
1980—Paul Conrad, Los Angeles Times
1981—Paul Conrad, Los Angeles Times
1982—Dick Locher, Chicago Tribune
1983—Rob Lawlor, Philadelphia Daily News
1984—Mike Lane, Baltimore Evening Sun
1985—Doug Marlette, Charlotte Observer
1986—Mike Keefe, Denver Post

NATIONAL HEADLINERS
CLUB AWARD
EDITORIAL CARTOON

1938—C.D. Batchelor, New York Daily News
1939—John Knott, Dallas News
1940—Herbert Block, Newspaper Enterprise Association
1941—Charles H. Sykes, Philadelphia Evening Ledger
1942—Jerry Doyle, Philadelphia Record
1943— Vaughn Shoemaker, Chicago Daily News
1944—Roy Justus, Sioux City Journal
1945—F.O. Alexander, Philadelphia Bulletin
1946—Hank Barrow, Associated Press
1947—Cy Hungerford, Pittsburgh Post-Gazette
1948—Tom Little, Nashville Tennessean
1949—Bruce Russell, Los Angeles Times
1950—Dorman Smith, Newspaper Enterprise Association
1951—C.G. Werner, Indianapolis Star
1952—John Fischetti, Newspaper Enterprise Association
1953—James T. Berryman and Gib Crocket, Washington Star
1954—Scott Long, Minneapolis Tribune
1955—Leo Thiele, Los Angeles Mirror-News
1956—John Milt Morris, Associated Press
1957—Frank Miller, Des Moines Register
1958—Burris Jenkins, Jr., New York Journal-American
1959—Karl Hubenthal, Los Angeles Examiner
1960—Don Hesse, St. Louis Globe-Democrat
1961—L.D. Warren, Cincinnati Enquirer
1962—Franklin Morse, Los Angeles Mirror
1963—Charles Bissell, Nashville Tennessean
1964—Lou Grant, Oakland Tribune
1965—Merle R. Tingley, London (Ont.) Free Press
1966—Hugh Haynie, Louisville Courier-Journal
1967—Jim Berry, Newspaper Enterprise Association
1968—Warren King, New York News
1969—Larry Barton, Toledo Blade
1970—Bill Crawford, Newspaper Enterprise Association
1971—Ray Osrin, Cleveland Plain Dealer
1972—Jacob Burck, Chicago Sun-Times
1973—Ranan Lurie, New York Times
1974—Tom Darcy, Newsday
1975—Bill Sanders, Milwaukee Journal
1976—No award given
1977—Paul Szep, Boston Globe
1978—Dwane Powell, Raleigh News and Observer
1979—Pat Oliphant, Washington Star
1980—Don Wright, Miami News
1981—Bill Garner, Memphis Commercial Appeal
1982—Mike Peters, Dayton Daily News
1983—Doug Marlette, Charlotte Observer
1984—Steve Benson, Arizona Republic
1985—Bill Day, Detroit Free Press
1986—Mike Keefe, Denver Post
1987—Mike Peters, Dayton Daily News

PULITZER PRIZE EDITORIAL CARTOON

1922—Rollin Kirby, New York World
1924—J.N. Darling, New York Herald Tribune
1925—Rollin Kirby, New York World
1926—D.R. Fitzpatrick, St. Louis Post-Dispatch
1927—Nelson Harding, Brooklyn Eagle
1928—Nelson Harding, Brooklyn Eagle
1929—Rollin Kirby, New York World
1930—Charles Macauley, Brooklyn Eagle
1931—Edmund Duffy, Baltimore Sun
1932—John T. McCutcheon, Chicago Tribune
1933—H.M. Talburt, Washington Daily News
1934—Edmund Duffy, Baltimore Sun
1935—Ross A. Lewis, Milwaukee Journal
1937—C.D. Batchelor, New York Daily News
1938—Vaughn Shoemaker, Chicago Daily News
1939—Charles G. Werner, Daily Oklahoman
1940—Edmund Duffy, Baltimore Sun
1941—Jacob Burck, Chicago Times
1942—Herbert L. Block, Newspaper Enterprise Association
1943—Jay N. Darling, New York Herald Tribune
1944—Clifford K. Berryman, Washington Star
1945—Bill Mauldin, United Feature Syndicate
1946—Bruce Russell, Los Angeles Times
1947—Vaughn Shoemaker, Chicago Daily News
1948—Reuben L. (Rube) Goldberg, New York Sun
1949—Lute Pease, Newark Evening News
1950—James T. Berryman, Washington Star
1951—Reginald W. Manning, Arizona Republic
1952—Fred L. Packer, New York Mirror
1953—Edward D. Kuekes, Cleveland Plain Dealer
1954—Herbert L. Block, Washington Post
1955—Daniel R. Fitzpatrick, St. Louis Post-Dispatch
1956—Robert York, Louisville Times
1957—Tom Little, Nashville Tennessean
1958—Bruce M. Shanks, Buffalo Evening News
1959—Bill Mauldin, St. Louis Post-Dispatch
1961—Carey Orr, Chicago Tribune
1962—Edmund S. Valtman, Hartford Times
1963—Frank Miller, Des Moines Register
1964—Paul Conrad, Denver Post
1966—Don Wright, Miami News
1967—Patrick B. Oliphant, Denver Post
1968—Eugene Gray Payne, Charlotte Observer
1969—John Fischetti, Chicago Daily News
1970—Thomas F. Darcy, Newsday
1971—Paul Conrad, Los Angeles Times
1972—Jeffrey K. MacNelly, Richmond News Leader
1974—Paul Szep, Boston Globe
1975—Garry Trudeau, Universal Press Syndicate
1976—Tony Auth, Philadelphia Enquirer
1977—Paul Szep, Boston Globe
1978—Jeff MacNelly, Richmond News Leader
1979—Herbert Block, Washington Post
1980—Don Wright, Miami News
1981—Mike Peters, Dayton Daily News
1982—Ben Sargent, Austin American-Statesman
1983—Dick Locher, Chicago Tribune
1984—Paul Conrad, Los Angeles Times
1985—Jeff MacNelly, Chicago Tribune
1986—Jules Feiffer, Universal Press Syndicate
1987—Berke Breathed, Washington Post Writers Group
NOTE: Pulitzer was not given 1923, 1936, 1960, 1965, and 1973.

NATIONAL NEWSPAPER AWARD / CANADA EDITORIAL CARTOON

1949—Jack Boothe, Toronto Globe and Mail
1950—James G. Reidford, Montreal Star
1951—Len Norris, Vancouver Sun
1952—Robert La Palme, Le Devoir, Montreal
1953—Robert W. Chambers, Halifax Chronicle-Herald
1954—John Collins, Montreal Gazette
1955—Merle R. Tingley, London Free Press
1956—James G. Reidford, Toronto Globe and Mail
1957—James G. Reidford, Toronto Globe and Mail
1958—Raoul Hunter, Le Soleil, Quebec
1959—Duncan Macpherson, Toronto Star
1960—Duncan Macpherson, Toronto Star
1961—Ed McNally, Montreal Star
1962—Duncan Macpherson, Toronto Star
1963—Jan Kamienski, Winnipeg Tribune
1964—Ed McNally, Montreal Star
1965—Duncan Macpherson, Toronto Star
1966—Robert W. Chambers, Halifax Chronicle-Herald
1967—Raoul Hunter, Le Soleil, Quebec
1968—Roy Peterson, Vancouver Sun
1969—Edward Uluschak, Edmonton Journal
1970—Duncan Macpherson, Toronto Daily Star
1971—Yardley Jones, Toronto Star
1972—Duncan Macpherson, Toronto Star
1973—John Collins, Montreal Gazette
1974—Blaine, Hamilton Spectator
1975—Roy Peterson, Vancouver Sun
1976—Andy Donato, Toronto Sun
1977—Terry Mosher, Montreal Gazette
1978—Terry Mosher, Montreal Gazette
1979—Edd Uluschak, Edmonton Journal
1980—Vic Roschkov, Toronto Star
1981—Tom Innes, Calgary Herald
1982—Blaine, Hamilton Spectator
1983—Dale Cummings, Winnipeg Free Press
1984—Roy Peterson, Vancouver Sun
1985—Ed Franklin, Toronto Globe and Mail
1986—Brian Gable, Regina Leader Post

Index

INDEX